THIS SIMPLE GAME

THE KEN BARNES STORY

AS TOLD TO JIMMY WAGG

First published in 2005

EMPIRE PUBLICATIONS
1 Newton Street, Manchester M1 1HW
copyright Ken Barnes and Jimmy Wagg 2005

ISBN 1 901 746 49 6

Cover photograph: courtesy of the author
Cover design and layout: Ashley Shaw
Edited by Ashley Shaw and Stuart Fish
Typeset in Gill Sans and Minion
Printed in Great Britain by Antony Rowe Ltd., Chippenham, Wilts.

CONTENTS

ACKNOWLEDGMENTS

June and Debbie for their patience. Peter Barnes and Brian Hughes for their encouragement. Everyone who contributed, but especially Franny Lee for smiling when my son dropped an ice lolly down the back of his couch. Stella, the labrador, for her doorstep welcome. My kids, Louise and Joe, for the incipient poverty that led me to embark on this venture and, of course, Ken himself for the hours of stories and laughter(not to mention the experience of being smoke cured).

JIMMY WAGG

Jimmy Wagg was born in a little fishing village called Hulme, in 1953. Aged 10, he moved to another village, just outside Wilmslow, called Wythenshawe.

Educated at St.Bede's College and then Sheffield University, he has worked as a freelance broadcaster with BBC GMR since the late 80s. He won a prestigious Sony Award, in 1995 for a live broadcast following the death of Sir Matt Busby.

He now lives with his partner, Debbie, and kids, Louise and Joe, in Timperley. However, the yearning for village life is deeply engrained and the family are planning to sell the house (don't tell the Council) and head for a life in Penury.

By the way, he's a City fan.

FOREWORD

I am absolutely delighted that Ken Barnes has decided to tell the story of his life in football, because he has made a huge contribution to the game and to Manchester City.

Ken and I go back a long way. In fact, the first two games of football I ever saw on TV were the '55 and '56 FA Cup Finals and he played in both. He was an excellent player; very intelligent, very creative. I loved to watch him. He's often described as the best wing-half never to play for England and I wouldn't argue with that.I know the great Sir Matt Busby rated him very highly and there's no finer accolade than that.

I got to know him personally a few years later. He took me under his wing when I went to City as a teenager. Okay, Manchester wasn't New York, but when you come from Aberdeen via Huddersfield, it's nice to have someone to look out for you. Not out on the pitch so much, but as a new kid in the big city. He took me out and showed me the best places to go in the town. He couldn't have done more for me. He even taught me to drive. He was a real friend to me back then and he still is now.

Ken has an incredible knowledge of the game. He also has a great passion for it. Even when he stopped playing, he never lost that love and enthusiasm. I never had the desire to be too involved once my playing days were over. That said, it was hard not to get passionate when you got talking to Ken. His office at Maine Road became the stuff of legend, of course. I loved it there. It was on my way into Manchester and I couldn't resist calling in. You were guaranteed a cup of tea and a chance to talk about football - getting away was the hard bit! You had to have Ken's seal of approval though. I don't remember seeing too many directors in there.

Ken is one of the straightest and most trustworthy people I've ever known. People used to beat a path to his door if they needed to talk. Senior pros or young kids, it made no difference. If you needed to talk to someone you could trust implicitly, Ken was that man. He cared about people and he cared about the club. If you talk to any of the kids he signed, you'll hear it in their voices; genuine affection and real respect. In fact, you'll hear it in the voice of anyone lucky enough to know him.

I could talk forever about Ken the player and about Ken the man, but let me sum it up like this; Ken Barnes is one of the best guys in the world.

Denis Law
Manchester
September 2005

THIS SIMPLE GAME

It used to be an easy game, a simple game to play,
Twenty - two men, a ball, some posts and the game was underway,
Wingers played wide, forwards attacked, defenders tried to defend
Halfbacks supported attack and defence; the game went from end to
*   end*
Then some bright spark said: "changes must come, let's find some
*   ideas to poach*
The players are entertaining too much" and so they invented the
*   coach*
They set up a course at Lilleshall on "how to kill the game"
To take part you had to be boring and dull, uninteresting and tame
They thought and they thought these little grey men and many new
*   ideas were sought*
and so, instead of playing to win, how not to lose was taught
Initiative must be quelled at birth, each team must play to a plan
The ball must go to the side, or back, if forward then drop the man
Then they invented the POMO line, what's that for Heaven's sake?
Well, they had to think of something new, for spectators were still
*   awake*
And when they've emptied all the grounds (for that seems to be their
*   aim)*
Maybe they'll finally realise - it was such a simple game!

Anon

The above poem might not have caused too many sleepless nights for William Shakespeare, but Ken feels it does strike a chord with those of similar beliefs to himself, about the merits of coaching.

KEN BARNES

THE FOOTBALL FACTS AND FIGURES OF HIS LIFE
IN THE PROFESSIONAL RANKS

Joined Manchester City from Stafford Rangers on May 8th
   1950.

League debut against Derby County on January 5th 1952.

Regular first team football from start of 1954/55 season.

Played 257 league, 23 FA Cup and 1 League Cup game for the
   club, scoring 18 League and 1 FA Cup goals.

Joined Wrexham as player - manager in May 1961.

Returned to Maine Road on August 27th 1970 as a member of
   the coaching staff.

Chief Scout from 1974.

In 1986 Manchester City won the FA Youth Cup and 8 of that
   side, all signed by Ken, went on to play for the first team at
   Maine Road.

In 1992 Ken was sacked (or advised to retire!) by Peter Reid.

Returned under Brian Horton as a part time scout.

2000 sacked by Joe Royle.

2005 Inducted into the Manchester City Hall of Fame.

CURRENTLY KEN IS highly involved in grassroots and school football in Malaysia, where he has become a one of the game's best known figures.

Ken Barnes won an FA Cup Winners Medal in 1956, having won an FA Cup runners-up medal in 1955. He played for the Football League Team and for the England "B" team, but never won a full England cap.

These are the bald facts and figures of Ken's career in professional football. Of themselves, they are a very poor indication of a truly remarkable contribution, made by one man over a period of 50 years, to the game and to Manchester City. I hope the following pages will go some way to show how he became an integral part of the Blues over half a century. I hope they will also provide an insight into a turbulent, but endlessly fascinating, period in the history of the club.

I have only had the chance to get to know Ken in recent years, so I have enlisted the help of the players, managers, scouts, fans and friends who have shared his time in the game, to help to tell his story and to offer their personal opinions of the man and his contribution to City in particular and the game in general. Every single person I asked to talk about Ken was eager to do so and that surely speaks volumes for his standing amongst the people who know him best.

What follows is a chronological account of Ken Barnes' involvement with the game of football, from childhood to the present day. I thought it would be interesting to pause the narrative at certain points, to allow those people involved with him, at those stages of his career, to offer their thoughts on, and stories about, Ken.

Because Ken holds such strident views on certain aspects of the game, the final few chapters of this book give rein to his passionate opinions on such issues as coaching, youth development and the future of the game.

NB. Ken has been known to use the odd swear word in the course of his working life and his use of the vernacular is reflected in the following pages - what my old mum used to call "bad language". It's not coming out, so decide for yourself if you want to come in!

INTRODUCTION

For kids who've grown up in an age of video games, mobile phones and the internet, it's all but impossible to conceive a world where TV was still a rumour and even radio was a new fangled notion. You do not have to be far over 40, though, to recall a time when leisure, for the young at least, was dominated by outdoor pleasures rather than microchips. For generations of working class boys, growing up in the cities and towns of Britain, that meant football.

Ken Barnes was, and in many ways remains, one of those boys. Born in Birmingham, slap bang between the two World Wars, Ken's early life followed a pattern that is instantly recognisable to legions of footballers throughout the early part of the twentieth century.

Looking back over nearly 70 years, some of his memories of inner - city childhood may have blurred around the edges, but he still talks with a passion about the 'street academies' where he learned to play the game. He also recalls, with immense fondness, the after school kick-abouts that would start at 2 aside, grow to resemble the crowd scenes in *Ben Hur* and then shrink back again. He believes fervently that those back street games and the hours and hours of unwitting practise that went with them were the seed beds of the professional game in this country. The vast majority of those hundreds of thousands of young footballers would never be more than enthusiastic amateurs, but for the gifted, those lads blessed with real ability, the groundwork had been laid amongst those rows of terraced houses.

The world has changed of course, and in a purely material sense, undoubtedly for the better. Ken, though, believes that from a footballing perspective, something precious has been lost from the game and, quite possibly, lost irretrievably.

Ken Barnes was widely regarded as one of the finest footballers of his generation and after a distinguished playing career with Manchester City throughout the 1950s, he spent nearly a decade away from Maine Road before returning to work for the Blues, in coaching and scouting roles, for a further 30 years.

He holds forthright views on the game, especially when it comes to the subject of coaching. But before anyone dismisses what he has to say as the 'in my day' rantings of another embittered former pro, let me remind you that his integrity and knowledge of the game saw him serve under every Manchester City manager from Joe Mercer to Joe Royle.

Away from football, Ken is described as a 'character'. Make of that what you will. That may be a tale for another day. This is the story of Ken's life in football. I'm honoured, and privileged, that he asked me to help him tell it.

PART ONE

THE EARLY YEARS

Ken Barnes was born on March 16th 1929 in the Small Heath area of Birmingham, in the shadow of St. Andrews, home of Birmingham City. Although the start of his own time as a professional footballer was still 20 years away, the game ran in the family - his uncle, John Shepherd, having played for Birmingham in the 1920s. Although Ken would never become an avid devotee of the club, he watched them on a regular basis with his father and whenever he played against them in later life, especially at St. Andrews, the game would always evoke memories of his childhood.

Ken's early life was absolutely typical of a working class lad growing up in a major industrial city. Apart from a spell in the army his father, Herbert, worked all his life on the railways. His mother, Leah, looked after the family before the war but, after starting war work at SU Carburettors, went on to be a union delegate at their factory in the city. Ken had two younger sisters, Hazel and Susan:

"We were a close family, I suppose, but very ordinary really. Our life seemed to be just like everyone else's. Most dads headed off to work in the morning and it was the mothers who were really the central figures - certainly as far as the kids were concerned. Your dad went to work, you ran to your mother if you needed something".

When Ken was six or seven years old, the family moved a few miles to Yardley. His memories of school are hazy on the academic front, but as early as junior school, football was already starting to be a dominant factor in his young life. He captained Audley Road to victory in the Birmingham Eastern Area Shield - a day he still recalls with pride, "Of course, your first trophy, at any level, is a bit special. I was lucky enough to go on and win an FA Cup winner's medal at Wembley, but I don't remember being any prouder than I was as captain of the school team that won the Shield. As young lads, that was our FA Cup Final, a very special day for us all."

By this time, Ken had already accepted that football, rather than scholastic excellence, was to be his driving force:

"I did alright at school, I suppose. In fact, I was house captain and a senior prefect, so I did care and I did apply myself, but if I'm being really honest, more than anything else I loved to play football. Most of the lads I palled about with were just the same - I had a couple of good pals, Barton Foster and Bernard Munford, and we were all the same, we would play football all day, every day, if we could. We really were football daft. Football wasn't our hobby, oh no, it was more than that - much more. It may sound odd to some people, but it was more a way of life. It was an obsession, but not just for us, thousands and thousands of lads were exactly the same. Every school and every street in every town was its own school of excellence. There were no cars, so we took over the street. We practised all day every day, we really did, and never realised we were doing it. Mind you, you had to learn quickly - when you play twenty-a-side and you make a mistake, you don't get another kick for half an hour.

"Looking back, life was a lot simpler back then. Your whole life played out within a few streets. You didn't travel or anything. There was no telly, so there was no real idea of comparing what you had with other people. You had what you had - end of story. My dad went to work, my mother ran the home; that was my life and pretty much life for everyone I knew. In that life, kids played in the streets and for boys that meant football. That was all there was, we never questioned it. With the benefit of hindsight, of course, you can see that it was incredibly intensive. If you ran a football club for kids these days, and wanted the lads to put in the hours that we did, you'd have social services all over you. You'd never be allowed to get away with it. We played for hours and hours. If we had a ball that was great, if not we'd make one out of rags or paper. Or we'd even play using a stone, as long as we were playing. We wouldn't have wanted it any other way, the game was our obsession."

When he wasn't playing the game, Ken was watching it. As mentioned, he used to go to St. Andrews with his dad. Entry to the ground was usually by a system known to cash strapped football fans the world over. Dad paid for himself and young Ken squeezed through the turnstile with him for free. He was enthralled by the game and loved to watch the top players of the day:

"I had my favourites, of course I did. I used to love to watch Ambrose Mulrayney and George Edwards at Birmingham and at the Villa I watched out for Frankie Broome and Eric Houghton. I also loved Harry Hibbs, Fred Harris and Billy Hughes. Happy days."

Ken moved onto Lea Village school to continue his education, but the backdrop to life as a reluctant scholar cum budding footballer was about to change with the outbreak of the Second World War.

HITLER AND A CHICKEN

World War 2 may have dominated the lives of adults at the time, but Ken Barnes remembers the war more as a backdrop to his everyday life, rather than as an all consuming event. He was just 10 years old when it started and recalls the impact of the conflict through the eyes of the child he was. Of course there were changes to be faced. His father was in the army reserve and was immediately posted to France, leaving schoolboy Ken as the man of the house. Mother Leah started on war work and Ken's grandmother looked after Ken and his sister. Air raid sirens meant another sleepless night huddled under the stairs for the Barnes family - uncomfortable, but preferable to the flooded Andersen shelter in the garden.

To those of us with no experience of war, the very idea of being bombed might be something to occupy a high percentage of our waking thoughts. However, Ken's clearest memories of the time were of the impact of the war on his football - he *was* only a child!:

"Organised football seemed to go out of the window, so we had to grab every chance we could to have a kick-about. If the all clear sounded and there was a clear space to play, we played. You didn't know when you'd get the chance again, so off we went and fuck the Luftwaffe!"

It may seem strange to generations who have grown up in the electronic age, but for Ken and hundreds of thousands of kids like him in the big cities, the war was something remote. Yes, there were air raids and rationing and other privations, but in a time of no television and no foreign travel, certainly for working class kids, the conflict was not played out live on the box in the living room and the fighting was happening somewhere mysterious called 'abroad'. With the resilience of children, Ken and his contemporaries adapted to their changed circumstances:

"Of course we were aware there was a war on, but we were just kids. You don't look at the big picture when you're that age. We didn't analyse or think too much about things, because kids don't. It might seem strange to people who didn't live through it, that we weren't constantly fretting about Nazi paratroopers or whatever, but kids do see things in very simple terms. We didn't think of the war as some noble battle for the future of civilisation - did we bollocks - no, we saw it as something that cocked up our football. That's how it was and how it should be. Kids are kids, they live in their own little world and it's quite right that they should. They're not meant to worry about things.

"What's the point of being a kid if you're meant to think about adult things? Even today, for all their computers and mobile phones and designer clothes, kids still live in a very small world really. It might seem very grown up and sophisticated to be sending e-mails to the other side of the world or whatever, but do you really think their world reaches much further than their friends and what's happening in the next ten minutes? Does it balls. As kids, ours didn't and theirs doesn't. The world might change, but I'm pretty sure that the way kids see it, it doesn't.

"Funnily enough, one of my clearest memories of the war, was when my mother asked me to kill a chicken. We kept a few to help out with rationing. Bloody hell, I remember trying to kill the bugger - what a bloody job that was! It would certainly come as a shock to the kids of today, who think chicken is born shrink wrapped! It's funny really, you live through something like that - one of the most important times in history - and the thing you remember best is trying to kill a bloody chicken!"

When his father was invalided out of the army with duodenal ulcers, life resumed a kind of normality in the Barnes household and normality for Ken meant playing football. In the absence of organised football in the schools, Ken and his friends played for Flaxley Rangers, as well as seizing every opportunity for an impromptu kick-about.

So, even in wartime, a pattern emerged and Ken did get to play his beloved football. In 1943, the approach of Ken's 14th birthday was the signal for another landmark in his life. Time to leave school and work for a living.

THIS WORKING LIFE

Fourteen years old and time for young Ken Barnes to find a job. His first steps into employment were to coincide with rapid strides in his football progress.

He started working for the Post Office in 1943, at a factory employing some 1200 people on Fordrough Lane in Bordesley Green, where he was set to work assembling switchboard components. The basic pay was 17 shillings and sixpence per week and he gave the lot to his mum, who gave him two and six back as pocket money. Within weeks, Ken's footballing skills saw him playing for the works team against grown men:

"I did okay, I suppose. I held my own. I got a few lumps and bruises to show for it mind, but I did alright. You have to remember, of course, there were no such things as age groups back then. You were 14, out in the adult world, and you had to compete on those terms. You played because you wanted to play and it was the old adage; if you were good enough, you were old enough. Whatever level you play at though, professional or amateur, if you're the new kid, the older lads are always going to test you out, to see what you're made of. There was never any question of taking it easy because I was only a kid. No way. If I wanted to be out there, and I did, I could expect to take what was coming, and there was plenty, fuck me there was.

"It was the same in a kick-about. As soon as the hooter went for a break, you could bet that someone would be out in the yard with a ball. It was only a brew time kick-about, but no one was taking prisoners. At dinnertime, every day, it was the same thing; bolt down your dinner and get playing till it was time to get back to work. To the modern observer, it might look a bit harsh, kids mixing it with grown men, but it wasn't just football, it was life. You left school at 14 and you learned to live in the adult world. You learned your trade and you learned your football. Work and football - that was my life really, and to be fair, life for most working class lads who'd left school. Who knows what might have happened if I'd grown up in the modern age of computers and such. Maybe I'd have sat up in my bedroom staring at a screen all day. But that wasn't my world. Work and play on grown up terms. Of course it was hard, but I tell you something, we learned the best way possible; by practising every hour that God sent."

As with school, Ken remembers work primarily as a backdrop to playing football. Within a year, Ken had been asked to play for Moor Green, the leading amateur side in the Midlands, and had made the first team on a regular basis by sixteen. This might still be amateur football, but of a very good standard. Despite his breakneck rise at amateur level, Ken is adamant that, at this stage, he had no thoughts of being a professional player:

"I just got out there and played. I never gave it a thought as a possible career, I honestly didn't, though you had to be pleased to be playing at such a good club. Sadly, amateur football is viewed as a bit of a backwater nowadays. People think anyone with talent is bound to be attached to a professional club. Back then, the top amateur clubs had real status. To be playing in the first team for Moor Green was a real feather in my football cap, it really was. They had a nice ground and a couple of thousand would turn up to watch. The top amateur sides were still recruiting grounds for professional clubs. It's not like today. Back then they'd actually sign amateurs on. Clubs like Moor Green, Bishop Auckland and Barnet were very highly regarded. They're all still going, but, unfortunately, the respect for that level of the game seems to have gone by the board. All I know is, it gave me the chance to play with some bloody good players, I can tell you, and as a consequence, I really felt that I was learning all the time."

Ken insists there was no great career path - just the desire to spend as much time as possible on the football field. But what would a psychologist have made of the fact that, after Ken's first week in gainful employment, he headed to W Shillcock Ltd in Birmingham, to order his first ever pair of made to measure football boots. He might have had no thoughts of being a professional, but he was going to be an amateur with style:

"It's funny the things you do. Made to measure boots, bloody hell. It doesn't seem like much, I suppose, to modern kids. They probably wouldn't bother to play if they didn't have a pair of boots that cost an arm and a leg. It was a bit more of a big thing back in the 1940s. The kids who had any football boots at all, would usually have hand-me-downs. If they were too big, you stuffed them with paper. If they were too small, you just had to live with it. It was a different world back then, but, that said, the basic instinct is probably the same today. Your first pay packet, the first money that you've earned in a real job, you want to mark it in some way. Whether it was ordering made to measure boots back then, or a mobile phone now. I reckon most youngsters feel the urge to splash out a bit when they get their hands on their own money for the first time. It's one of the marker posts on your way to being an adult. For someone like me, who was football daft, obsessed with the game, the idea of made to measure football boots was irresistible."

Along with progress in his amateur football, Ken had the first inkling of a professional interest in his talent, when he received a letter from Birmingham City asking him to play for their Colts side:

"It was okay I suppose. I don't remember being that excited, though I suppose I must have been. I was quite intrigued really, as to how they knew about me. I never did find out. I didn't see it as a great opportunity or anything. It was just a chance to play football with good players. Looking back, I suppose it does seem a bit impersonal, doesn't it? Just a letter. But as I've said before, what did I have to compare it with? I'd never been approached by a professional club before, so I could hardly turn round and say that the club usually send someone round in person, could I?"

So now Ken was part of a professional set-up, but it was a very different football age. Contact between the Colts and Ken took the form of weekly postcards, telling him what time to be where every Saturday:

"You turned up and played and then went home again and waited for the next card. Nobody told you anything. Nobody told you how you'd done or gave you advice. You did your best and hoped you'd get another card. There were no training sessions. I carried on training with Moor Green. It really was a different world. I'd been in work long enough to know that you had to do things on other people's terms - that was life for lads like me. I don't remember anyone ever asking me what time I fancied turning up for work! You played by their rules. Youngsters weren't given guidance back then. Looking back it was tough, but that's the way it was. I had nothing to compare it with, other than more of the same, so I just got on with it. It was a case of sink or swim."

Ken swam. Nobody told him if he was impressing or improving, but the cards kept dropping through the letterbox. Maybe a career with his home town club was beckoning, but fate stepped in. Ken's friends were still playing regularly for Flaxley Rangers, who were due to play in the Aston Villa Cup. They asked Ken to turn out for the big game, but it clashed with a match he was down to play for the Birmingham City Colts. Ken decided to play for Flaxley. Rangers won and his friends were, understandably, delighted. But he had not bothered to tell Birmingham he would not be playing for them and the postcards stopped with immediate effect. Birmingham's loss was to prove to be Manchester City's eventual gain, but Ken's dad, Herbert, was less than impressed;

"My old fella was livid, bloody hell he was. He told me how stupid I'd been and that opportunity might only ever knock once. But as I saw it, I hadn't seen my mates for a while and it was a really important game for them. I felt I couldn't let them down. When you look at it from an adult point of view, it was a bloody stupid thing to do, no doubt about it. But, it's like I've said before, you don't see the bigger picture when you're young. I didn't bother trying that line of argument with my dad though, because he wasn't listening."

As his father's wrath subsided, Ken settled into a routine of work and football; the Post Office and Moor Green. But it wasn't long before the professional game took another look at his developing talent.

GET SOME IN!

Ray Westwood had been a star of the Bolton team of the 1930s. He had been part of the "Wartime Wanderers", who had all enlisted together at the start of the Second World War. A player of no mean quality himself, Westwood saw Ken Barnes playing for Moor Green, recognised a burgeoning talent and recommended him to the Burnden Park club.

Ken was back on the fringes of the professional game. Although it was by no means easy, travelling by train and bus from the Midlands to Bolton on a regular basis. Eventually, it became an accepted part of his footballing routine. Work for the Post Office, train with Moor Green and play for Bolton's 'A' team:

"I enjoyed the playing side of things - but then I always did, at any level. The travelling was a bind, but it had to be done. It became part of my life. There was no point in whingeing about it. If I wanted to have a go with Bolton, then the travelling was part and parcel. What could I have done differently? Should I have told them I'd only play for them if they had a game in Birmingham? The truth back then was that the clubs called the shots and if you wanted to give it a go, you did it on their terms - end of story. I must have done alright, because they kept picking me, but there was no feedback. There was no coaching or such like. You just assumed that if they kept picking you, you were doing more right than wrong, but nobody ever said fuck all. That was the way it was back then, not just for me, for everyone. I don't remember being bothered about it. I wasn't desperate for someone to tell me how to play. Even as a youngster, I believed that if you could play, you just got on with it.

"You learnt a few things from more experienced players, of course you did, but you weren't waiting for someone to sit you down in front of a bloody blackboard and draw you a diagram. Let's face it, whatever level you play at, you pretty well know if you've done alright. I never felt I was struggling to cope or to keep up or anything. I pretty much knew I was good enough to be there. I hope that doesn't sound too big headed, but I think I would have known if I'd been out of my depth. I don't think I'm the type to kid myself, and anyway they kept asking me back, and back then, they weren't doing that out of sentiment. If I hadn't been up to the mark, the letters would have stopped, make no mistake."

In March 1947, Ken Barnes celebrated his 18th birthday. A milestone for any youngster, it had another significance in those days - National Service. It was time for Ken Barnes to get some in:

"I don't remember having very strong feelings one way or the other about doing National Service. I was only going to Stafford, for fuck's sake. I travelled further than that every weekend to play football. I just got on with it. It was what you did when you got to eighteen, so off I went. If I was concerned about anything, it was only about how it would affect my football."

Not too badly as it turned out. Like school and work before it, National Service was to be what Ken did when he wasn't playing football. Still, in service of King and Country, he duly found himself stationed at RAF Stafford (16 MU) and working in the stores. His on-field abilities were quickly recognised and appreciated and Ken ended up playing so much football, that it's safe to say, if the balloon had gone up, he would not have been there to catch it.

Along with his footballing endeavours for the RAF, Ken continued to play for Bolton Wanderers at weekends. His immediate superior was a keen fan of the game and saw a talent way beyond the everyday in his new recruit. He was happy to help that talent blossom, by arranging for Ken to be free for weekend games at Burnden Park. To enhance his enjoyment, Ken played regular midweek football for the camp team and he was finding life to be so close to football heaven, that he was actually considering signing on for a further 10 years:

"I really did think about a long term career with the RAF. From where I was standing, life was just about bloody perfect. I was getting fed, boarded and paid and I was certainly playing more football than I was raffing. It was like being a pro really. I got to play with some good lads and some good footballers. I was young, healthy, fit as a flea, with money in my pocket and I was allowed to keep a foothold in the professional game with Bolton. You tell me any football-daft lad, from my background, who wouldn't have wanted to keep that going. At that age you don't give a thought to 10 years from now, do you? When you're 18, 10 years is a lifetime that can never pass. You tell me an 18 year-old who believes he'll ever be 30. When you're that age, getting old is like dying; it only happens to other people. I thought about the time I was having and, like any kid of that age, I really believed it would never have to end."

Then, inadvertently, Bolton Wanderers put a spanner in the works by making a formal request for the use of Ken's services to the Camp Commander. Permission was denied and the informal arrangement, that had suited all parties, was over. By now, Ken had taken the express route through the service's football structure and was playing for the RAF team itself, with the likes of Roy Swinburn and Jimmy Wardaugh. As such, he was far too precious a commodity to be allowed to fritter away his weekends playing for a professional club. His country, or at least the RAF team, needed him.

Bolton backed off, though they did keep tabs on Ken and actually came back in for him when his National Service was completed, only to find he'd already signed for someone else; non-league Stafford Rangers.

FROM STAFFORD TO MANCHESTER

Having guested for Stafford Rangers during the latter part of his National Service, Ken signed pro terms with them when his time in uniform was up. Again, the basis of his judgement was not long term football ambition, "The manager at Rangers, Billy Frith, had been at Coventry. I enjoyed my time there and when they offered me terms, I said 'yes'.

"I didn't think about Bolton coming back in for me. I'd started a new job at SU Carburettors, where the money was better than the Post Office, I played for Stafford at weekend and still trained with Moor Green. It seemed like a pretty good arrangement to me. Mind you, I must say, my dad was livid. He was convinced I'd set my sights too low. He gave me a right earful, he really did. People now might think it's strange that I didn't look for a chance at a bigger club, especially after my time at Bolton before, but things were a lot more fluid between pro and semi-pro back then. There were some pretty decent players at Rangers as I recall. I didn't give too much thought as to whether I should be aiming for a higher level. I did what I've always done; if I was enjoying myself, and I was, I just got on with it. There were no big plans or strategies, just a game of football to be enjoyed. Besides, with a good day job, I had to think of the money. My dad didn't half go mad though."

His dad needn't have worried. The big clubs had long since realised that Ken had the ability to play at a higher level. Birmingham City, Aston Villa and Sheffield Wednesday, as well as Manchester City, were keen to recruit the 20 year-old. In the end, Ken opted for the Sky Blues. Again, the reasoning was not based on any long term career strategy, "I spoke to Wilf Wild and Walter Smith from City. They seemed like nice people and, anyway, they had just been relegated, so I thought I might get more of a chance with them. They offered me £7 a week in the season, £6 a week in the closed season. I took it.

"I signed the standard 12 month contract, without even visiting the club. It makes me laugh when I read about modern players signing five-year deals. Don't get me wrong, I don't begrudge them what they get, though it has gone a bit mad of late, but when I think of how it was when I signed my first pro contract, well bloody hell. You got 12 months and each year the club decided whose contract would be renewed. At first you didn't think about it, but once you had responsibilities, or if you'd been injured or if you were just getting a bit long in the tooth, it was a nerve wracking time. Bloody hell, it did get very edgy as your contract came up. They held all the cards, they really did. We were bloody slaves really. It was okay when you were young and on your game, but every year a lot of pros would be sweating it out, waiting to see the retained list.

"These days I have to smile, when I read about some 30 odd year old signing a four-year deal. Good luck to them, I wouldn't wish the contractual set up we had on anyone, but back then you'd be 30 and sweating to see if the club would deign to offer you another year. Nowadays, players want lucrative deals to take them through their thirties. Let's face it, if you can get an agent to squeeze an extra year or two out of a club, why should you worry if you never kick a ball? You still get to top up your savings by a million or two.

"Anyway, I'd gone for City and I was off to Maine Road. I'd only ever been through Manchester on my way to Bolton. I certainly didn't know where Moss Side was. I think the fee was around £300, I'm pretty certain it wasn't as high as a thousand. I didn't speak to the other clubs. I didn't want all that mucking about. At least my dad was pleased. He thought it would have been hard for me, as a local lad, if I'd gone to Birmingham or Villa. You have to remember, of course, there were no agents back then, playing one club off against another for the best deal. I liked the people, I signed a contract. I know it might sound strange to people used to all the shenanigans that go on nowadays, but it really was a different world - so I just went with my instincts, I honestly did. I thought that if these were the people running the club, they'd do for me. Ironically enough, once I got there, the manager Les McDowall and I never really got on. Maybe if I'd met him first I'd have gone somewhere else - who knows?"

It may not have been fate, but it was certainly not calculation; Ken Barnes was now a professional footballer with Manchester City.

PART TWO

EARLY FRUSTRATIONS

It's 2005. A young player joins one of the country's biggest clubs, having been snapped up from under the noses of several other top sides chasing his services. After the usual whirl of press and TV interviews, he quickly leafs through a luxury car magazine and circles his possible choices. Before being taken to see his Cheshire penthouse, he has meetings with the club's PR man, followed by his dietician, psychologist and then his media coach. Tomorrow, his agent has scheduled a meeting with a potential boot sponsor about a 6 figure deal...

Wind back 50 odd years and a 20 year-old Ken Barnes disembarks at Piccadilly train station, his wordly possessions contained in a pressed cardboard case, and finds his way, on the bus, across Manchester to his digs on the corner of Lloyd Street and Platt Lane. He was put up with the Clayton family and was sharing with two other young players, Dave Ewing and Spencer Evans.

The next morning, Mr Clayton points young Ken in the direction of Maine Road, before heading off to work at Reynolds Chains. Ken makes the short walk to the ground - his first ever visit:

"I didn't feel particularly nervous, as I remember. I walked along Lloyd Street and turned right towards the stadium. It was my first proper look at Maine Road. I must say the size of the place knocked me back a bit at first. Like most big city grounds back then, it was tucked in amongst rows of terraced houses, so when you turned up the road and caught your first glimpse, the ground looked bloody massive, towering above everything else around. Just for a second, it took my breath away. It was certainly exciting and maybe a little bit daunting, if I'm honest. But I knew I wanted to be there - absolutely I did.

"There were a few press lads there. Not for me, of course, they were after Roy Paul, who joined at the same time. Still, I got on the pictures. I suppose that if a player of the stature of Roy Paul was signing for City today, there would be a real media frenzy. Television, radio, press. It was a lot more low key back then. Remember, it was only five years after the war had finished. Maybe there was still a bit of perspective left. The modern day hype hadn't started. Of course, the football writers were there, but it wasn't like it would be now, like a royal wedding or something.

"It was funny in some ways, because Roy was one of the greats, a Welsh international at his peak. I was a kid just starting out, but we hit it off right from the start. So much so, that a couple of years later, he was Best Man at my wedding. We stayed friends all through the years until he died recently, even though I didn't get to see him all that often. I still tell anyone who'll listen, just how good he was. I'd heard of him before I went to Maine Road, of course, but until I got the chance to see him and play with him first hand, I never realised just how good a footballer he was. Phenomenal."

Ken met Fred Tilson, who was in charge of the reserves, and after that it was the typical first day blur of faces:

"I remember thinking that I was going to give it my best shot. Being away from home didn't throw me, because I'd just done two years National Service, but I decided that I wouldn't go back home for a while - I wanted to really throw myself into it. It took about a month to settle, as I recall. It took me that long to find a routine. Although I'd only been training part-time, I found professional training okay. My stamina had always been good. I wasn't fast, but I could run all day. We used to train from 10 till 12.30 and then we went to eat. Afternoon training was optional. Training was pretty routine really, but it could be bloody hard, I can tell you. The emphasis was on physical fitness. Some mornings we never stopped running. I felt I was on personal terms with every bleedin' pebble on the running track round Maine Road.

"We also used to run up and down the terracing for half an hour and then do a whole bloody range of exercises. Twice a week there were full scale practice matches involving the first team and the reserves; first team attack and reserve team defence against reserve attack and first team defence. On Friday we did sprint training. We used to wear the old style running spikes. We never trained with a ball on Fridays. It was a widely held belief at the time that that would make you hungry for the ball come Saturday. As for coaching and guidance, there was next to nothing really. You learnt by playing, especially by playing with good players. You weren't told what to do and, to be honest, I didn't want to be told. You took responsibilty for what you did on the pitch. You didn't want someone to tell you how to play. If you couldn't play, what the fuck were you doing being a pro?"

Ken found his feet quickly at Maine Road, though, at this point, the first team was still a yawning gulf away:

"The first team was something different altogether. They were treated differently - as an elite if you like. It was the done thing to knock on the first team dressing room door. You didn't just walk in."

He progressed, in short order, from playing with the 'A' team to the reserves, and adapted to life as a full time pro. Away from football, Ken found Manchester to be a very lively place:

"I couldn't believe it - every pub had a resident pianist and singer. The whole city was one big night club. When my dad came to visit, he was astounded. Compared with Birmingham, certainly the part of Birmingham where we lived, there was so much going on. I met my first wife, Jean, in the Parkside pub on Lloyd Street and, I can remember, Frank Swift used to get up and give them a song in there. The relationship between players and the public was so different back then. Of course some of the players were well known, but it wasn't the kind of superstardom of today. Don't forget, a lot players would be on the same bus as the fans going to the game, so if you saw Swifty singing in a pub, it didn't cause a riot like it would now, if you saw Wayne Rooney or Shaun Wright-Phillips doing a turn! You could go out and very few people knew who you were. You weren't on the telly all the bloody time. Alright, some of the players would be recognised, but by no means all of us. If you were in a pub, people didn't go running to phone the papers. People didn't bother you. We used to go out to a pub or the pictures, no problem. Could you imagine that today?

"It's funny how things have changed. Nowadays, the players earn such vast fortunes in the higher reaches of the game, they live a life that is totally different to the fans. Back in the 50s, we were well paid compared to the average man, certainly. We used to earn three or four times the average wage. What would that be today? If the average wage is, say, £400, we'd be getting between £1200 and £1600. That's great money, obviously, but when you hear of players earning, 50, 60, 70 or 80 thousand pounds a week, it shows you how things have changed. I always thought it was a real privilege to be paid to play football and it was, I suppose, a glamorous job in some ways. But we didn't have boot deals and the like. Yes, we lived in the nicer parts of the city, but we lived in the same areas as the fans. I suppose we'd all have mansions out in Cheshire these days.

"I've always said that I do not begrudge modern-day players earning a good living, because it's a short career for most people. Bloody hell though, it has gone a bit crazy, if I'm being honest."

Back in those regimented times, the players were issued with a code of conduct - a guideline, if you will, to the proprieties of life as a professional player. But, as young fit men of any generation are liable to do, Ken and his contemporaries were liberal in their interpretation of the rules:

"No alcohol after Wednesday? I never saw the problem of a couple of halves on a Friday, if it helped you relax before a game. It was a matter of common sense really. It was strange how we were left pretty much to our own devices as footballers, but told what to do when we weren't actually playing."

As Ken settled to life at Manchester City, he began to feel frustrated about his lack of progress towards the first team. Ken might not have been one for making career plans, but by now he was convinced he was good enough to be given a chance. The club had bounced back from relegation at the first time of asking in 1951, but even with the club back in the top flight, Ken believed that he was at least the equal of those ahead of him the in the wing-half pecking order:

"It was a very frustrating time - I really thought I was ready. I don't want to sound big headed, but I really did think I could do a better job that some who were getting a chance."

The problem was exacerbated by the fact that Ken and the manager, Les McDowall, didn't get on particularly well:

"We were very different animals. I really believe that he did spend a lot of time thinking about the game, but, the trouble was, he didn't bother to tell you what he was thinking. He found it hard to communicate with people - certainly with me. We were chalk and cheese really. I liked a bit of a laugh and he was very standoffish. He'd walk past you without seeming to notice you were there. I used to shout over to him - just to force him to respond, really. But he never told me why he didn't pick me. Never. I suppose that's just the way it was back then. But even by the standards of the 50s, McDowall was a remote figure. He picked the team and as for everything else, well, you made it up once you got out there."

Finally, in January 1952, Ken got the call to first team colours against Derby County at Maine Road. The Blues won 4-2:

"I was bit nervous in the first half, but did okay in the second. After a win like that, you feel you might be given another go. Alright, I hadn't exactly ripped up trees, but I'd not made a fool of myself either. I hadn't felt out of place and having had a taste, I was ready for more. It was like the genie was out of the bottle. Let's face it, I was nearly 23, I'd been pretty patient so far, but now I wanted to prove myself and I thought a convincing win would be enough to get me another chance."

He was immediately dropped and nobody offered a word of explanation. Frustrated beyond belief, Ken put in a transfer request. This was met with a terse "Okay" from McDowall. Ken went on the list and did not kick another ball for the club, at any level, for 3 months:

"I had bloody splinters in my arse from all that time I spent watching from the stand."

With no move forthcoming, he went to see the manager and asked to come off the list. He was back in the reserve side for the following game. Oldham Athletic manager George Hardwick had wanted to sign Ken, but City had asked for a £1500 transfer fee, which had proved too rich for the Latics.

With Ken increasingly of a mind that his future might lie away from Maine Road, Les McDowall introduced a tactical innovation to the first team, that would finally allow the wing-half's talent to reach full bloom on the senior stage at Manchester City - the Revie Plan.

HUNGARIANS MY ARSE!

Over the years, the Revie Plan has acquired almost mythical status amongst fans of Manchester City - certainly amongst those of a more mature vintage. The popular conception is that the Blues manager of the time, Les McDowall, had looked at the way the Hungarian side had destroyed England at Wembley in 1953, by utilising a deep-lying centre-forward. McDowall had then adapted the idea for use at Manchester City. After honing the system in the reserves, he introduced it into the first team and then pulled the masterstroke of linking Don Revie and Ken Barnes as the pivotal characters in his revolutionary new plan. The press at the time were very much taken with the idea, and dubbed City "The Magyars of Maine Road". This widely held view of how the Revie Plan came into being, is dismissed by Ken Barnes as "bollocks":

"It had fuck all to do with the Hungarians. We were playing a deep-lying centre-forward in the City reserves, before they turned England over at Wembley. Johnny Williamson was a smashing inside-forward in the reserves and he got moved to centre-forward. Johnny had an inside-forward's instincts to come deep and link up with the half backs. Back then, a centre-half expected to mark a centre-forward and a centre-forward meant a spearhead, someone looking to get in the box at every opportunity - not someone disappearing towards the half-way line. Back then, I suppose, roles were a bit more regimented and when Johnny dropped off, the opposing centre-half didn't know whether to stick or twist. It suited me down to the ground. I could push forward and try to exploit the confusion. Traditionally, a wing-half had been seen, first and foremost, as a defender. Now I had the chance to do what I was best at. I wasn't the best defensively, but I like to think I could create things going forward. That was my strength, or at least I believed it was.

"If I'm honest, the system came about more by accident than planning. Johnny got moved to centre-forward to cover an injury, as I recall. The rest just happened and then we saw a chance to make something of it. It was all a bit of something and nothing really, but other teams just didn't get to grips with it. It worked though. We went over 30 matches without losing. But I'm telling you straight, we were doing it before the Hungarians got here and the idea that it was a tactical gem from McDowall is nonsense. When he watched us playing the system with the reserves, he wasn't impressed. In fact, I remember him saying we'd never get away with it in the First Division. Les McDowall's masterplan? Do me a favour. There's more shit talked about the Revie Plan than just about anything I've been involved with in the game - except coaching of course!"

At the time, Ken was still frustrated at his failure to break into the first team:

"I tried not to let it affect my game, but I looked at people like Jock McTavish and Bill Spurdle and honestly thought I was as good, or even better than them. That might sound big headed, but I really couldn't see why I wasn't getting my chance. Needless to say, nobody ever offered any kind of explanation."

Ken's frustration was about to end. At the start of the '54/55 season, Les McDowall decided, for whatever reason, that the time was right to take the deep-lying centre-forward system onto the First Division stage. The withdrawn centre-forward role was given to Don Revie, a player summed up by Ken Barnes as "quality" and Jock McTavish was to be the attacking wing-half. The first game of the season was away to Preston North End and the Blues were drubbed 5-0. Don Revie's post match comment to Les McDowall was short and to the point:

"If you want this to work, you need Ken Barnes in the team."

The following Wednesday, Sheffield United were the visitors to Maine Road. Ken was at right-half and City won 5-2. It was the start of an 11-game run, in which the Blues would lose only once, away to Cardiff City. After nearly four and a half years, Ken Barnes was finally given the chance he'd craved. He seized the opportunity and became, to most observers, the pivotal player in the Revie plan.

It was a massively important season for Ken personally. After marking time for so long, he had finally made the crucial breakthrough to regular first team football. It was an important season for the club as well. After three indifferent years back in the top flight, City went on to finish 7th in the league and to reach the FA Cup Final against Newcastle United.

THE ROAD TO WEMBLEY

Having played a major role in Manchester City's improved league form, Ken Barnes was also part of an FA Cup run that saw the Blues all the way to the final at Wembley.

In the third round City were away to Derby County. The Baseball Ground was renowned in the 70s for its very poor playing surface. Former Nottingham Forest and Everton star Duncan McKenzie summed it up better than most:

"If you won the toss, you kicked towards the shallow end!"

Things were no better back in the 50s. It was not a pitch best suited to the skills of Ken Barnes:

"It was a shithole, a bloody awful place to try and play. My instincts were always to get the ball down and pass it. I was usually wasting my time there and it wasn't just me. Anyone who had the idea that football was best played on the ground, would never relish a trip to the Baseball Ground. You could all but guarantee that a third round tie, at the start of January, would be hard going. It was hard going, but there were other factors in play that day, from my personal perspective. It was my first FA Cup game and I scored my first ever goal for City, so it was a pretty good day for me.

"The goal was a bit special, and not just because it was my first for the club. I got the ball about twenty yards outside our box and set off forward. The movement ahead of me was tremendous, but every time I weighed up the pass, it just seemed to open up for me. Next thing, I'm on the edge of their box and let fly, bang, my first goal for the club. I was ecstatic, but I suppose it was the type of situation where a modern day coach would have given me a bollocking for not releasing it. Or maybe for carrying it and not letting the ball do the work or some such. It was good enough for me though. Derby were nothing special - hard working but ordinary. We expected to beat them and we did, 3-1. Joe Hayes and Don Revie scored the others. All round, I think you would have described it as a job well done - with a little bit of icing on the cake for me personally."

The fourth round draw saw the Blues first out of the bag against arch-rivals Manchester United. A Maine Road derby in the FA Cup - a tie to fire the imagination and a massive crowd of 74,723 turned up to see it:

"It was the kind of game you dream of playing in as a professional footballer; a cup derby against United, in a stadium so packed you couldn't hear yourself think. Bloody marvellous. We were on the up and up and they were supposed to be the best side in the country. We had the Indian sign on them that year, though. We won all three games, including 5-0 at their place. It was unbelievable. Funnily enough, the thing I remember most about the cup game, was that their centre-half, Allenby Chilton, got sent off. They get sent off for anything nowadays, of course, but back then it was still a rarity. You usually had to have a corpse, or a least the chalk outline of where the corpse had been, to see a sending off. I don't remember the tackle being anything that you didn't see week in and week out back then. In fact, I was close by as it happened and I told the referee not to send him off. Allenby Chilton was a fine player. He might have been coming towards the end of his career, but he wasn't just a stopper, he could play a bit as well. We won 2-0, Joe and Don with the goals. It was a terrific day for us.

"Round 5 was away to Luton Town in a blizzard. Bloody awful to play in and the pitch was an absolute mess. It was one of those games you were just glad to see the back of. Nobby Clarke scored twice as I recall. The weather sticks in my mind more than the game itself, but it was another round safely negotiated.

"In round 6 we were drawn away to Birmingham City. It was a dream tie for me, in many ways. For four years, I'd barely had a sniff at City and now I was back at St Andrews in the FA Cup quarter-final. I had to bloody pinch myself. Can you imagine how it felt for me to go there in those circumstances? Bloody marvellous. There were nearly 60,000 in the ground. It was a really hard game. We won it with a late goal, but I just remember it wasn't a place for the faint hearted out there. Johnny Hart got on the end of a Nobby Clarke free-kick towards the end. I was glad to hear the final whistle, I can tell you. But then it dawned on me that we were in the semi-final and at that moment you forget the kicks and bruises, and we were all covered in them, you just enjoy the feeling. It really was a hard game though. And it was truly a bit special for a Brummy like me to win there, in such an important match.

"I couldn't wait to hear the draw for the semi - final. We got Sunderland at Villa Park and Sunderland meant Len Shackleton. Len was a wonderful player and a real character as well. He had so much talent, he could make you look a fool. He was unstoppable when he was at his best and not above a bit of piss-taking. He liked to get the crowd going. The type of player the fans love, but most modern coaches would probably hate.

"As for the game itself, well, it should never have been played, I can tell you that. There is not a cat in hell's chance it would have gone ahead these days. It had pissed down all day Friday and again on Saturday morning. When we got to the stadium, the place was already heaving. The streets around the stadium were packed with fans. When I walked out and looked at the pitch, there were great areas under water. Nowadays, the ref would not have needed to look twice, it would have been off. I think he must have been under an amazing amount of pressure to go ahead though. All those people at the stadium. Remember as well, Birmingham wasn't just a quick jaunt down the motorway back then and as for getting there from Sunderland, well, it was a real trek. So it didn't really surprise me that they decided to get it played. I didn't fancy my chances too much. You can't play it on the deck through bloody great puddles. The best you could do was to play chipped passes around the lakes of water. Except for Len Shack, of course. Bugger me, he just flicked the ball up and juggled it through the water. An FA Cup semi - final and he's playing keepy fuckin' uppy!

"It did stop raining and some of the water drained, but it was like a mudbath. We got the rub of the green on the day and Nobby scored a header about ten minutes into the second half. It was a day for grit and determination rather than great football. I remember that our defence were tremendous on the day. Big Dave Ewing was a giant in that match. It was his type of game really. It might not have been a classic, but we were at Wembley. Can you imagine how I felt? Before the season, I was thinking I might have to leave to get a chance at first team football. A few months later, I'm in the first team, I've scored my first senior goal and now I'm set to play in the biggest club final in the world. Bloody marvellous really, when you think about it."

Nowadays, The FA Cup may be losing some of its glamour for the top clubs, with the increasing precedence of European football. But in 1955 it was very different:

"Jesus, every pro dreamt of playing in the Cup Final at Wembley. Every fan dreamt of going to London and seeing the Twin Towers as they walked along Wembley Way. It was such a prestigious thing for a player to be part of. Nowadays, the Cup seems to be a bit of a sideshow for some of the very top clubs. The Champions League seems to be the thing they want to be involved in. I suppose it's understandable in some ways. Europe is seen as the ultimate test for a top team now. Back then, it was Europe that was still the sideshow, so the Cup really was seen as something very special. As for me, I thought I must be dreaming. It was my first time at Wembley. The sad thing is that you're concentrating so hard on what you have to do, you just don't have time to savour the occasion, to take it all in. There wasn't the same media frenzy back then of course, but bloody hell, you knew it was special. Very special indeed."

Sadly, for Ken and his team mates, the perfect end to the season was not to be. The Blues were a goal down after just 45 seconds when Jackie Milburn scored for the Magpies and then came the hammer blow of losing Jimmy Meadows, very early in the game, with a damaged knee. In the days before substitutes, ten-man City were always going to struggle on the wide open spaces of Wembley, though Bobby Johnstone did equalise before Newcastle went on to win the game 3-1.

After the game, Roy Paul said that the Blues would be back to win the Cup the following year, as indeed they were. Ken's memories of the time do not echo the public defiance of his captain:

"I was very dejected - to come so far and end up with nothing. I remember thinking that nobody remembers the losers and that a chance like this might never come my way again. As it turned out, of course, I didn't have to wait long. At the time though, blimey, you really did think this could be your only go at it and now the chance was gone. When we got back to Manchester, the fans gave us a great reception. I think they realised that we'd done our best and that the odds had been stacked against us once we lost Jimmy."

The record books may show a year of ultimate disappointment

for Manchester City, but there can be no doubt that the 1954/ 55 season had been the most important, so far, in the footballing life of Ken Barnes. After the years of frustration, he was now not only an established part of the City set-up, but also a vital one. Moreover, he'd had the chance to play in the final of the most famous club knockout competition in the world. Not bad for a player who, less a year before, had been contemplating a move from Maine Road. Roll on 55/56!

A GREAT SET OF LADS

After the great personal success of 54/55, it is not surprising that Ken Barnes could hardly wait to get started again. After a pre-season tour, the new campaign started with a two-all draw at home to Aston Villa, followed by a 7-2 thumping at Wolves. Hardly the start the Blues were looking for, but beating Manchester United 1-0 at Maine Road, in the first derby of the season, was guaranteed to cheer the City supporters. A terrific unbeaten run in the league, from the end of January through to mid March, along with progress in the FA Cup, led to talk of the double. Sadly however, the league form tailed off and City finished fourth. The side was definitely making progress, but the fact that Manchester United went on to win the title, rather took the sheen of that particular achievement:

"It was a bit disappointing to miss out in the League, I suppose, but I really felt I was part of a bloody good team, well, we showed that in the Cup, didn't we? We had some lads who would have graced any side really. Obviously we've lost a few over the years, but I'm still good pals with some of them and I see Paddy Fagan and Johnny Williamson at the ground on match days. There were some fine players and some right characters in that side, bloody hell, there were!

"Bert Trautmann was as good a keeper as I have ever seen. He took to English football so well and it certainly wasn't easy to be a German in this country so soon after the war. For people who didn't experience it, it's hard to explain what life was like for Bert in the years just after the war. Can you imagine how some of the Jewish fans of the club felt when City signed a German keeper? It was all still so raw and fresh in the minds of people. To his credit, not just as player but also as a man, Bert overcame all that and now he's greeted like royalty whenever he comes back to Manchester, and quite rightly so. Bert and me got on really well together - still do, as a matter of fact. We used to travel to Maine Road together on match days. As a keeper, he was magnificent. I don't think he had a weakness. For me, he was the best I ever saw or played with, no question. If there was a better keeper, I'd love to have seen him.

"Jimmy Meadows was an excellent player, an England international. Sadly, he never got back from the knee injury he suffered in the '55 Final. I remember Bill Leivers replacing him. Bill was having a moan one day, saying I was getting forward so much, I was leaving him exposed. I told him straight: "Jimmy Meadows got capped for England playing behind me." That shut him up for a bit!

"Dave Ewing - 'Pull up at Dave's'- was an old fashioned centre-half. He could be very, very rugged, but not much got past him, I can tell you. No nonsense defensively, Dave was the first to admit that he wasn't the best on the ball. He knew his job and stuck to it.

"Roy Paul was the captain and what a player he was. He was so bloody powerful, just awe inspiring at times. Brilliant in the air, two good feet, great control. He was more about power than guile perhaps, but what a truly marvellous asset for any side. He had such a presence out on the park, he was a born leader. I can still see him now. In his pomp, he was awesome, just awesome. He joined the club at the same time as me, if you remember. I was the novice, he was a Welsh international, ten years older than me, but we hit it off and he was the best man at my wedding. Top class as a player and as a man.

"Then there was little Bobby Johnstone. What can I say, what can anyone say, about the little man? On his day, he was, quite simply, the best I ever played with. Very clever, very astute, wonderful control and could score goals. He wasn't a grafter, but what talent. Jimmy Murphy, the assistant manager at Manchester United back then, loved Bobby as a player and he wasn't a bad judge was he? Off the park he was a bit of a bugger, though. He certainly liked a drink. I remember once, we played Portsmouth on New Years Day at Maine Road. Bobby came in looking fuckin' awful. He'd been out celebrating Hogmanay till God knows what time. He asked me to sneak him some aspirin for his thick head without the trainer seeing. He was in a right state. I had to point him down the tunnel towards the pitch. I didn't think he had a cat in hell's chance of getting through the game, never mind playing any serious part in it and then, fuck me, he goes out and scores a hat trick - all headers! I wouldn't mind, but I'm sure he was still half pissed when he came off after the game.

"I couldn't bloody believe what I'd seen. He sat there in the dressing room after the game, like the cat with the fuckin' cream, but what could you say after what he'd done? I shouted to him:

"Hey you, you little Scotch ****! You'd better go out and get pissed every fuckin' week!"

"I wouldn't mind, but he had a bad knee by the time he came to City, so we'll never know how good he would have been fully fit. There are so many little tales about Bobby and just how good he was. What a player - bloody marvellous. He really could do it all. We were practising one day and Bobby told a very young Colin Barlow that if he could deliver a corner at the right height, he'd volley it past Bert Trautmann from the edge of the penalty area. You should have seen Bert's face - fuck me!

Talk about if looks could kill. It was like a red rag to a bull for Bert. Anyway, young Colin crosses the perfect corner and, bugger me, Bobby volleys into the net. Bert got nowhere near it. Absolutely unstoppable. Bert glared at him and said: "You couldn't do that again if you tried it a hundred times." Well, Bobby shouted to Colin: "Same again, son." Blow me, over it comes and Bobby smashes it past Bert again. Bert didn't speak to him for a week. That was Bobby, an unbelievable talent at times.

"Don Revie was quality. A great player and a great man. He was always very meticulous and he's always remembered, I suppose, for his dossiers on the opposition when he was manager at Leeds. I collared him once about that. He looked a bit sheepish. What a lot of people might not know is that, by the end of his time in management, he had changed to the point where he just told them to get out there and play. When I first took over as chief scout at City, I went over to Elland Road to see Don, to pick up any tips or advice. He was only too pleased to help me and pulled out his scouting form. Fuckin' hell! It had all these sections - left foot, right foot, heading, control, pace - honestly, it went on forever. I went through it for ages and then turned back to Don. I let him sweat for a minute, because I knew he wanted my opinion on the form:

'What do you think Ken?'

'Very impressive Don, but you've missed a question out.'

'Missed a question out? What's that Ken?'

'Can the laddie play?'

"Don was a shrewd character, but his public image was at odds with the man. In the media, he was known as a calculating manager, cold even, but that was nothing like the reality. Like all great managers, he was very protective of his players and knew all the staff at Elland Road right down to the tea ladies. He took a genuine interest in their welfare and he never forgot his friends. That said, he always had a realistic view of life.

When he left City after the Cup win to go to Sunderland, he called to see me. We had an interesting conversation:

'Don, why are you going to fuckin' Sunderland? We've just won the FA Cup for God's sake. You've played for England - what are you moving for?'

'Ken, tell me this. When it's all over, how will you know if you've had a good career?'

'I'm not sure what you're getting at Don.'

'Ken, if you want to know if you've had a good career, look at your bank balance.'

"That makes him sound very mercenary, but playing in the times we did, he realised that you were a long time finished and the game didn't usually want to know you when your playing days were over. Of course, the idea of Don as a mercenary was reinforced when he left the England job to go to the Middle East. Bloody hell, the papers had a field day, but Don was just being Don. He had his sources in the FA. He knew they were after getting him out. He just decided to do it on his own terms. I know his image is cast in stone for a lot of people, especially after the England thing. But you ask the players who played with him, or the players who played for him, what he was like and you'll get a very different story. Especially once he got rid of those bleedin' dossiers.

"Joe Hayes was an out and out finisher. He didn't put too much into his all-round game and never seemed to give it a moment's thought once the final whistle blew. He scored plenty of goals for City, but I always thought Joe could have done a lot more, if his attitude had been different. It takes all sorts, of course, but I really got the impression that Joe's only interest in football was that ninety minutes out on the park. When the final whistle went, he put football back in the cupboard till the next game.

"Roy Clarke - Nobby - is a nice man and was a fine, fine player. He could beat people, he had pace and he certainly had a wonderful left peg. But he had, and has, one fault. He could pull a fag, lit, out of his pocket! Seriously, Roy has been part of the fabric of Manchester City for half a century and has served the club wonderfully well down the years. Top class.

"Paddy Fagan - best two feet I've ever seen. Stunning power in either foot. An Irish international, like his father before him. A great fellah and terrific company. You won't meet a nicer man.

"Johnny Hart was a very intelligent player. Not flashy, but a good all round game. A good football man.

"Johnny Williamson could play the deep-lying centre-forward role as well as anyone. He had terrific control for a big man. I still see Johnny at home games. A smashing bloke, a real pal. I'll say it again, these were bloody marvellous players and I was privileged to be part of it."

Over his time at Manchester City, Ken gained a reputation as a practical joker, but he would qualify that:

"I think I was more of a piss-taker or wind-up merchant than a practical joker as such. It's always been part and parcel of football. Let's face it, it's that type of environment really, isn't it? Playing football for a living, it's like you never have to grow up. That's why footballers always seem a bit childish to some people, I suppose. It started with the carrot. If someone had a bad game, I used to stick a carrot on their clothes peg after the game. Nowadays they give you marks out of ten in the papers. We had a much simpler system. If you played like a donkey, you got a carrot.

"You also got to know who were the best people to wind up. Bert Trautmann was, and still is, one of my best friends and I still look forward to seeing him whenever he comes back to England. But Bert, like every goalie I've ever met, always fancied himself as an outfield player and he especially fancied himself at head tennis. We used to play all the time in the gym under the main stand at Maine Road and Bert took it deadly seriously. We all did, but for Bert, well, it really was that serious. Now Bert had been a prisoner of war in England and remember, being German in this country so soon after the war was not easy. It is to his credit that he won over the English fans, not just at City but all around the country, with his unbelievable ability. In these politically correct days, I don't suppose it would be the done thing to have a go at Bert about the war or his nationality, but back then it was seen as fair game.

"If Bert was getting a bit passionate about the head tennis, and especially if he was winning, I'd get him going by saying the ball was out when it was quite clearly in. Well, Bert would start fuming and insist it was in and I'd say it was definitely out and then start to call into question his, shall we say, Teutonic heritage. If I got it just right, he would blow his top and go storming out of the gym. He would reappear, a few minutes later, looking very sheepish. He was a great bloke Bert, but I could play him like a violin when it came to head tennis. The daft thing was that, even though he knew it was coming, he just couldn't stop himself rising to the bait. Maybe it was his competitive streak. But whatever it was, it suited me down to the ground for a wind-up. Like I said before, it probably looks very childish from the outside, but footballers are like big kids a lot of the time."

On a personal level, Ken Barnes was now firmly established as the first choice right-half at the club, and there was a growing campaign for him to be given his chance at international level. Whatever the press had to say, Ken himself took a more pragmatic view:

"Back then, the manager didn't pick a side for England, they still had a selection committee. I don't think bloody one of them had ever played the game at any serious level and they're telling the manager who'll be in his side for an international match! It seems ludicrous looking back. Actually, it didn't seem so bleeding clever even then. It used to amaze me, sometimes, it really did. I'll admit it used to stick in my throat when I heard some of the selections. I'm not saying they should have picked me necessarily, though I do think I would have been able to cope if I had got the call. But I was staggered at some of the players who did get caps, I really was. Amazing, bloody amazing. I don't want to sound cynical, but any fool could see how many players were picked from the clubs whose chairmen were on the selection committee. Then again, even if I'd got past the selection committee, the manager, Walter Winterbottom, and me weren't exactly a mutual appreciation society."

If there was a touch of frustration in terms of his international ambition, things couldn't have been much better at club level. If the '54/55 FA Cup run had ended in bitter disappointment for Ken, the '55/56 Cup campaign was to provide the highlight of his playing career.

BERT TRAUTMANN

Bert Trautmann is regarded by many as the finest goalkeeper ever to play for Manchester City. He's regarded by some, as the best keeper the world has ever seen. Bert and Ken became great friends and often travelled to Maine Road together. From a purely professional perspective, Bert was between the sticks throughout Ken Barnes' playing career with the Blues and is, consequently, better placed than most to assess Ken the player:

"Manchester City could not have done without him. He was the best schemer, the best reader and the best analyst I ever played with. He had unbelievable ability. For example, he couldn't tackle, but still usually came out with the ball and, in my opinion, he was the crucial man in the Revie Plan. Don was important, of

course, but Ken was the critical factor. "

Ken is often described as the best player of his generation never to play for his country. Bert believes that to be true:

"Absolutely. I can't remember, over so many years, who kept him out of the side, but Ken was worth a place - no doubt whatsoever. Maybe his face didn't fit. Ken was Ken. I think he's mellowed with age, but he never thought much of Walter Winterbottom. He has always been very attack-minded and he's always spoken his mind - that's the way he is. Maybe Ken would have ruffled a few too many feathers on the selection committee."

In terms of Ken's contribution to the City cause in a scouting and coaching capacity, Trautmann is not surprised that Ken found and helped nurture so much talent. Albeit that some of that talent would go on to find its fulfillment elsewhere other than at Manchester City:

"No surprise whatsoever. Ken Barnes should never have been allowed to leave the club in the first place. It was a different world back then, we were just numbers on the payroll, not real people. But anyone who knew the first thing about football could see that he had an amazing knowledge of the game. That should have been appreciated and used for the good of the club. Football was his life. To let all that knowledge go to Wrexham was just stupid. When he got back, he signed all that talent. No surprise in that, only that the club let so much of it leave so cheaply. A lot of them went on to great things. So what does that say about Ken's judgement of a player? Who was right in the end?"

Bert Trautmann is quite rightly regarded as a Blues legend, feted whenever he returns to Manchester. One of the highlights of a return visit is meeting up with his old team mates and it is obvious that he still holds Ken in the highest esteem, both as a footballer and a man:

"As a player, Ken had amazing ability, a wonderful talent. As a person he was always honest, genuine and likeable. He still is. He's got a bit more diplomatic with age maybe, but he's still Ken.

Let me tell you this. I had a wonderful career with Manchester City and 40 years and more after leaving, people still honour me here. But I can truly say, that it was an honour for me to play with Ken Barnes."

PADDY FAGAN

Paddy Fagan was a team mate of Ken Barnes at Manchester City. 50 years on, they are still friends and meet up on match days. An Irish International, like his father before him, Paddy was known in his playing days for the explosive power he possessed in either foot. Apart from the fact of their friendship, he has a great admiration for Ken Barnes; the man and the footballer:

"Ken was a great player with unbelievable know-how. He could read a game so well, he never gave you a ball that would put you in trouble. I always believed that you could have blindfolded Ken, stuck him out on the pitch, and he would have known where to go by instinct. Ken always hated coaching. I think that's because he was born with a tremendous natural instinct for the game and he also had the brain to soak up any lessons to be learned from playing with good players. Whatever it was, he developed an incredible knowledge of the game. You won't find anyone who knows more.

"Off the pitch, I think Ken himself would be the first to admit that he was easily led. I remember on a pre-season tour, Bobby Johnstone, who I think you would describe in modern parlance as a 'party animal', said he was going to stay up to see the sun rise every day we were there. Knowing what Bobby was like, most of us just groaned and let the comment pass. Not Ken, oh no, he thought it was a marvellous idea. When Bobby asked for volunteers for that particular mission, Ken was right at the front of the queue. Sometimes he was a lot smarter on the pitch than

he was off it.

"Ken is honest and straight and a great lad to have as a friend. Maybe he was too honest sometimes. If he had something to say, he said it. Maybe that was why he never got the full caps his talent deserved. Back in those days, he might have upset too many powerful people. It's a shame, because I'm sure he would have done brilliantly on the international stage."

A friendship that endures for half a century is its own best advocate, so the last word from Paddy goes back to Ken Barnes the footballer:

"A lot of people say Ken Barnes was the best wing-half in England, never to win a full England cap. I'll tell you now, they were wrong. He was the best wing-half in England, full stop."

JOHNNY WILLIAMSON

Johnny Williamson was a centre-forward at Manchester City in the early part of Ken's time at Maine Road. Johnny has been a friend of Ken's ever since their playing days together:

"Ken and me hit it off right from the start, and we've stayed friends ever since. Friendship apart, as a player he was one of the best, certainly, that I ever played with. He was such a great passer of the ball, he always gave it to you at the right time. He always wanted to get it down and play. It was foreign to him to put the ball out of play. As long as I've known him, he's always been sceptical of coaches and the whole coaching thing. We always used to say, isn't it funny how all the best coaches seem to work with the best players. Ken was one of those players, born with a gift for the game. Over the years, I've always told anyone who cared to listen, that you never knew how he good he was till you had to play against him.

"Ken was a great player, but he did come unstuck occasionally. I remember once, Stan Matthews was tearing us apart down *the right. Ken decided he knew how to fix it and told everyone he'd sort Stan out. He was convinced that Matthews was being given too much room to go outside the full back. Over goes Ken and gives the great man about two feet of space to go past him down the line. Needless to say, two feet was all he needed; Stan recognised a challenge when he saw one. He left Ken on his arse as he went past him on the outside. In fairness to Ken, when Stan was flying, he was just about unplayable. Ken didn't get it wrong very often, but he should have kept well clear of Matthews in that mood.*

"Ken is my type of man and definitely my type of footballer. He had an exceptional talent that deserved to be seen on the international stage. The fact that it wasn't, says a lot more about the system back then, than it does about Ken's ability as a footballer."

FRED EYRE

Fred Eyre has carved out a number of different careers both inside and outside the game of football. Since his playing career ended, he has enjoyed success in his stationery business, and also as a writer, after dinner speaker and as a football scout with various clubs including Sheffield United and Stockport County. Fred was a youngster looking to make his mark at Manchester City when Ken was captain of the first team:

"Ken has always been great with the kids - once they cut their way through the cigarette smoke! He always had time for you and took an interest in how you were doing with your football. That wasn't the case with every senior pro back then. He really was a wonderful player. Having watched him play, I understand why he has next to no time for coaching. I don't really think coaching is aimed at people with the talent that Ken was born with. That

type of talent is a gift, it can't be coached.

"*In my opinion, two of his greatest attributes were his outstanding knowledge of the game and his sheer love for it. I never played against Ken in his prime, and I should probably be glad about that, if I'm being honest. But when he was at Witton Albion as player-manager, I did get the chance to see him first hand. He must have been over 40, but I couldn't get near him - not a chance - and I was only in my mid 20s. A great player and a knowledge of the game that is second to none.*"

THE ROAD TO WEMBLEY GLORY

The 1956 FA Cup run began with a 3rd round home tie against Blackpool, and Blackpool meant Stan Matthews, who was still playing even though he was now past his 40th birthday. He was a character who intrigued Ken Barnes, as, indeed, he did generations of football fans everywhere. The grainy old footage of Matthews approaching ridiculously close to a wary full-back, before skipping past the baffled defender to deliver a perfectly weighted cross, is one of the game's enduring images:

"He was still a threat, a wonderful player. Stan was ahead of his time in many ways. He was really interested in diet and things, at a time when most of us never gave it a second thought. I remember he caught me eating a pork pie once and he gave me a right bollocking on why it was no good for me. I tried to look interested, but I still finished the pie though. He was obsessive about fitness and doing everything to improve his physical condition. Make no mistake, we were professional footballers and fit by any standard, but Stan was years ahead of his time. I found it a bit strange in some ways, I suppose. Apparently he had a toilet shaped like a horse's saddle, because he was convinced that that was the best position to let nature take its course. I wasn't convinced myself, like, but it seemed to work for him. He played till he was 50!"

The Saturday game was abandoned after 55 minutes due to fog and mud with the score at 1-1. The game was rescheduled for Wednesday afternoon with more than 42,000 at Maine Road to see the Blues go through 2-1, with goals from Jack Dyson and Bobby Johnstone.

In the 4th round City were drawn away to Southend. The pitch was covered with sand and cockleshells to help the drainage. Ken was definitely not impressed:

"Without a doubt, the worst pitch I ever played on in my life. If you hit the floor, you cut yourself to bloody ribbons. What a leveller. We did well to get through. Bert Trautmann was absolutely outstanding, bloody brilliant, and he needed to be. The papers called us the Cockleshell Heroes. Well, that's as maybe, but I was just glad to see the back of the fuckin' place. Even now, I think back to it and I can feel those bloody shells cutting into my knees." City went through 1-0 with Joe Hayes the scorer.

Into February and in round 5, Liverpool were the visitors to an icy Maine Road. Over 70,000 turned up to see the game end 0-0 in very difficult conditions. A further 57,000 were present at Anfield four days later, as the Blues squeezed through in controversial circumstances. City were leading 2-1 when Liverpool legend Billy Liddell looked to have scored a last gasp equaliser. The referee, though, was adamant that he'd already blown for full time. It was an incident that would have kept the TV panellists in work for months these days, but the 'goal' was ruled out and City were in the 6th round. Understandably the Anfield crowd was not best pleased:

"It was bloody bedlam! We heard the whistle okay. In fact, some of us were already shaking hands at the half-way line. But Billy was heading hell for leather towards the Kop. There was such a din, the crowd never heard the whistle. But there's no question it had blown. Obviously the fans weren't happy, but there was no doubt the game was over when he put it in."

Ken Barnes was obviously delighted to be in the quarter-finals, but had a certain sympathy for Liddell, a player he rated very highly:

"A bloody brilliant player. He could play anywhere in the front line - left or right, inside-forward or centre-forward. A real football brain, very sharp, no doubt about it. One of the true greats. Think of all the great players for Liverpool over the years and he was as good as any and better than most. One of their all time greats, without a shadow of a doubt. To top it all, he was a lovely man as well. For all that, the whistle had definitely gone!"

March 3rd and Everton were next up at Maine Road. FA Cup quarter-finals tend to generate a great atmosphere, but Ken remembers the day as being just a bit special:

"Bert Trautmann picked me up on the way to the ground, as he usually did. As soon as we arrived, we could feel the tension and the excitement in the air. I remember thinking to myself that it could be a special day, you could almost smell it. God, even now, thinking back I can feel it. It's nearly fifty years ago and it still makes the hair on the back of my neck stand up."

76,129 saw City come from a goal down to win 2-1 with goals from Hayes and Johnstone:

"It was a very tight game. They ran us ragged in the first half. The noise in the ground was unbelievable, a constant din. I never normally noticed the crowd noise too much, but that day, well, it was a bit special. Inspirational in fact. They really helped to keep us in it during the first half."

In the semi-final City took on Tottenham Hotspur. The North London side had had an indifferent league season and, in Ken's opinion, they were 'not a patch on the early 60s side'. Their main threat usually came through the craft of Northern Ireland international Danny Blanchflower. Following Roy

Paul's prophetic words after losing the '55 final, the Blues were not to be denied at Villa Park and went through to Wembley, courtesy of a first half goal from Bobby Johnstone.

May 5th 1956, the FA Cup Final against Birmingham City and a chance for Manchester City to expunge the bitter disappointment of losing the previous year. Ken Barnes clearly remembers the build up to the game:

"It was different this time around. I felt more confident. There was less fear of the unknown. I was determined to try and take it all in this time, because the year before had passed by in a blur. One thing for sure, I had no intention of losing again. I remembered '55 and how it felt to lose at Wembley and the fear that I might never the get the chance again. Well, I had got the chance and I was determined that this time would be different. I was coming home with a winner's medal and no bugger was going to stop me!"

At the stadium, Ken observed his usual pre-match ritual and lit up a cigarette. Les McDowall looked surprised and asked him what he was doing. Ken, as always, made his point:

"Look, I have a fag before every game, you know that. It keeps me calm. Playing at this place is bloody hard work - the expectation, the nerves can really drain you. They talk about the turf sapping your strength. Maybe it does, but not half as much as the occasion. Now let me have this bloody fag in peace."

In his pre-match team talk, manager McDowall gave Ken the job of picking up Birmingham's Peter Murphy, so restricting Ken's usual freedom to get forward and link up with his frontmen. He was not impressed:

"I looked McDowall in the face and asked him straight out: 'Do I man-mark Murphy or play my own game?' He never really answered, he just waffled on about making sure Murphy didn't score. I tried again. 'Do I stop him scoring for them, or do I play for us?' He just waffled on again and moved off.

Typical really."

Manchester City dominated the first 45 minutes and took an early lead through Joe Hayes, but Birmingham equalised and it was all-square at the break. As the players made the long walk to the Wembley dressing rooms at half time, Ken Barnes recalls a frank exchange with Don Revie:

'Where the fuck have you been, Ken?'

'You heard what McDowall said about me marking Murphy.'

'Bollocks to that, get up here and play.'"

Ken took Don's advice and did get up there and play. City ran out winners 3-1, with further goals from Jack Dyson and Bobby Johnstone. Ken had a hand in Jack Dyson's goal and knew the Blues had played well:

"We were excellent that day. It could have been 4 or 5, no danger. Without doubt, the best day of my life in football so far. It was impossible to put into words and do it justice. We had a big do in London. Alma Cogan, who was a big star at the time, sang a song. But the best thing was when we got back to Manchester. Albert Square was jammed. They gave us a welcome I'll never forget. The atmosphere was amazing, it was absolutely intoxicating. The whole square was a seething mass of people, not just in front of the Town Hall itself, but the whole square and the streets leading into it. The noise and the excitement took your breath away, it really did. Can you imagine how it felt for me? It had taken me so long to get a chance and now I've got an FA Cup winner's medal and I'm part of all this. Bloody marvellous. It really is so hard to put into words. I can feel it better than I can describe it. Funny though, I'd promised myself I'd soak it all up this time round, but the actual Cup Final day still passed in a blur.

"I suppose that, apart from the result, what most people remember about the Final in '56 was Bert breaking his neck. It happened with about fifteen minutes left and though Bert looked a bit groggy, it didn't seem too serious. Then it took ages for them to find out he'd actually fractured a bone. They didn't find anything at first, but he was really suffering. Then, by chance, he got put in touch with some top radiologist and it was him who found the fracture. In some ways, I think it was a relief to Bert. At least he knew then that there was a reason why he was having so much pain. We missed him for a big chunk of the following season."

It had been another important and successful season for Ken Barnes. At 27, he was playing for a side of proven quality, he'd won an FA Cup winner's medal and he was being spoken of as a possible international player. The football world looked to be there for the taking.

But City wouldn't be City if they stuck to the plan. Sadly, "the best day of my life in football so far", would prove to be a pinnacle, not a platform.

THIS FOOTBALL CITY

The 55/56 season ended with Manchester United as League Champions and Manchester City winners of the FA Cup.

"There were some bloody good players in this city, I can tell you. We had some great players. Bert Trautmann was the best goalie I ever saw. If there was one better, I'd love to have seen him. Roy Paul was magnificent; pace and power, two great feet, brilliant in the air, top class. And on his day, Bobby Johnstone was the best player I ever played with; so clever, so astute, wonderful control. He was unplayable at times - and he had a bad knee by the time he came to Maine Road!

"Across the way at Old Trafford, Jesus, they had some marvellous players. It's not fair to single anyone out really, but I have to say, little Eddie Coleman was one I always loved to watch. Bloody hell, what a player. Guile and craft personified.

Superb control, good passer, a bit of disguise and kidology. He was incredibly talented.

"Strangely enough, we always seemed to do really well against United in the derby matches back then. I remember once we were winning against them and I heard Matt Busby's assistant, Jimmy Murphy, shouting to Big Duncan Edwards to switch from left-half to inside-left to try to get them back in the game. Then, later, he moved him back again. I shouted over: "Go on Dunc, get back there son. You're doing fuck all up here!"

"Big Duncan! What a footballer he was, and such a nice lad as well. With us both being from the Midlands, we hit it off right from the start. I used to see him in town and we'd have a cup of coffee in the Kardomah and have a chat - a smashing laddie. He achieved so much and he died so young, you can only imagine what he might have gone on to do in the game, if he'd had the chance to play out his career. He was so strong and powerful, built like a tank and remember, he was still only a boy, even if he was playing for England. Maybe he didn't have the trickery of little Eddie, but his all round game was really marvellous. He didn't have a weakness. But, bloody hell, they had great players all over the park: Roger Byrne, David Pegg, Tommy Taylor - the list goes on and on.

"My special pal at United, though, was Dennis Viollet. Maybe it was because Dennis was a Blue as a kid, but whatever the reason, we became good friends and used to meet up in town. We stayed friends until Dennis died recently. In fact, he used to stay with me when he came back to England from America, where he'd made his home. After finishing playing, he did all his coaching badges. I used to pull his leg about it. I told him I knew he had to get the badges to get work, but to make sure he let it all go in one ear and out the other once he'd passed the badge. He told me, in later life, that he agreed with me about the value of coaching. He said that, in America, he just threw the kids a ball and told them to get on with it.

"As a player he was brilliant, really wonderful. Strangely enough, when people talk about the Busby Babes, somehow he seems to get overlooked. I don't know if it's because he survived Munich, or maybe because he moved on fairly soon afterwards to Stoke, but he doesn't always get a mention, or to be more exact, as much of a mention as his talent would warrant. Let me tell you, that in a very fine team, he was as good as anyone. My good friend John Doherty, who played with Dennis for United in the 50s, would pick him in his all-time great United side without a second thought, and there aren't many better judges of a player than John. Dennis was a very fine footballer. He was very cute and crafty on the park. You watched him and watched him, convinced you had him covered. He'd be sauntering about then, bang, he was gone and you were a goal down. Like all great strikers, he had that composure in the box. He seemed to have all the time in the world - and there's not a fuckin' coach in the world who can teach you that. He wasn't anything special in the air, but on the floor, well, he was so quick. He had great control, two good feet and he never, ever, panicked. What a finisher - one of the best ever. I'd put him up against anyone. He used to caress the ball into the net. He'd be priceless now, he really would.

"Like I said, both clubs had some great players. It was a special time to be a footballer in Manchester, it really was. Back at the end of the 55/56 season, if you looked at the two sides, it looked like Manchester was set to be the football capital of England. Sadly it didn't work out that way, of course. City lost some good players and brought in lesser players to replace them; 50 years in the game and I've never seen that work - not once.

"As for Munich, you can't put it into words, even now. They were great lads, our pals most of them, and suddenly they were gone. It was a tragedy for everyone who died, footballers and non - footballers, and their families. But as a player yourself, you can't help wondering, sometimes, just what they might have gone on to achieve. I mean, most of them were just kids when they died - wonderful players and lovely lads. Then gone. So sad"

Ken was to find out later that Matt Busby rated him so highly he wanted to take him to Old Trafford:

"Anyone being linked with a move to Manchester United back then had to be flattered. They were a wonderful team, but don't forget, I was playing for a more than fair side myself. Nothing ever came of it, so it's all ifs, ands and maybes. It's nice to know that Matt thought I was that good a player though.

"I remember when Matt told me to call him by his first name. It doesn't seem like a big deal now, but back then for the manager of a club like United to tell a player to call him by his first name, well, it was quite something. I never could quite bring myself to do it though. I used to get to his name and then just mumble. It's always fascinated me as to why Matt, with his standing in the game, would have said that to me. Maybe it was because he had played for City, in the same position as me, back in the 30s. Whatever the reason, it was a real honour and I do mean honour, I can tell you. In fact, it was Matt who recommended me for the Wrexham job as player-manager.

"Over the years, we met on various occasions, and I saw him just after he'd decided to step down. He'd moved upstairs and Wilf McGuinness was taking over. I remember asking him if it had been a hard decision to end his time as manager. He told me it hadn't been as hard as he thought it would be, because the game had changed so much: 'It all used to be so simple Ken, but now everyone keeps telling me how complicated it is.'

"He was always so kind to me. I took my sons, Keith and Peter, to Old Trafford once, to get the players' autographs. We only lived in Chorlton and it wasn't far. We were outside the ground and there must have been 50 or 60 people hanging about with us, waiting for the players to come out. After a while, Matt came out and a cheer went up. He smiled at the crowd and he was just walking away, when he caught sight of me with the boys. He asked me what I was doing there and I told him we were waiting for the players. Next thing I know, he took me and the boys into the dressing room and they got to meet the players and get the autographs. Now I'm sure people will say that Matt was bound to do that for a fellow pro and maybe they're right. All I know is that, in that crowd, he could have pretended not to notice me and gone about his business. Instead he took the time out to do a kindness for my sons and it was a day they'll never forget."

THE DECLINE

At the start of the '56/57 season, things could not have been much better for Ken Barnes. His England debut seemed only a matter of time, he was the proud owner of an FA Cup winner's medal and, at 27, he was now a lynchpin of a very good Manchester City side. Sadly for Ken, the expected further good times did not materialise and the team went into decline. Jimmy Meadows never got back from the knee injury sustained in the 1955 FA Cup Final. Roy Paul and Don Revie moved on. Johnny Hart and Jack Dyson suffered broken legs. Ken was made captain, following the departure of Roy Paul. He regarded it as an honour, but he knew things were on the slide:

"It was a very difficult time. It didn't happen overnight, of course. But over a couple of seasons, you just knew that the quality was going down. I don't want to sound cruel, but the players coming in were not as good as the men they'd been brought in to replace. In my opinion, only George Hannah was top quality. It was strange for me. I had always enjoyed my football, at whatever level I played, but as captain I hated to see the side going downhill. It began to feel like a job. I still had a tremendous loyalty to the club, despite the difficulties, and we still had our moments, but I think I'd expected more after winning the Cup."

Les McDowall continued his tactical innovation with the introduction of twin centre-backs. Keith Marsden would, nominally, be inside left, but then would immediately drop alongside Dave Ewing. Unfortunately, a tactic which was to become a mainstay of English football in later years, seemed to cause more problems than it solved when first introduced at Maine Road:

"We were playing Preston North End and trying to use the twin centre-backs system. Tommy Docherty, their right-half, couldn't believe his luck. There was no one marking him and he had no one to mark. He was like a kid in a sweet shop. I shouted over to him: 'Bloody hell Tom, you must have worn a pair of fuckin' boots out tonight, you've had so much of the ball!'"

City lost the game 6-1 and that was followed by a 9-2 defeat at West Brom. System abandoned.

For Ken Barnes, the post '56 seasons may have fallen short of expectations but, as ever with City, there were some memorable games and none more so than his hat-trick against Everton in December 1957 - all penalties!

Overseas trips were increasingly part of the life of a professional footballer in the late 50s. Ken was to discover that, if he'd failed as a player, he would not have had the option of a life on the ocean wave. A closed season tour of America and Canada had been arranged to help promote soccer on the North American continent and the Manchester City players duly arrived at Southampton for the crossing to New York. Ken was looking forward to seeing the Big Apple, especially as Len Shackleton had put him in touch with a friend in the city who was going to show Ken the sights. He had no inkling of the troubles in store as he stood on the dockside:

"Bloody hell, I stood there looking up at this ship and it looked as big as the Town Hall, it was the *Mauritania*, a 35,000 ton ocean liner. I was really excited. People jump on ships and planes to America all the time nowadays, but back then, it still seemed like a real adventure. We set off and after about half an hour I'm feeling really funny. I went up on deck for a bit of fresh air and this ship, that had looked massive in the dock, was bobbing about like a bloody cork. I felt worse, so I went back downstairs to get a drink. I remember asking one of the crew when it would stop rolling about and he just shrugged and said it might be like this all the way over, if we were unlucky. I spent six days in my bunk and never went outside the cabin once. I couldn't wait to get off that bloody boat.

"New York took my breath away. Shack's mate took me round. Bloody hell, all these famous places you'd heard of and now I was there looking at them. What I did find strange, though, was that you'd be in some really smart place in Manhattan and then, just a few hundreds yards away, you'd be in a neighbourhood that looked like a war zone.

"We went all over America, from east to west and then up into Canada. It was marvellous really; a chance to see all those places. We had a great time and then, all too soon, the day came to set off for home.

"I was stood on the deck as we sailed down the St Lawrence river, thinking how beautiful it all was and then we headed out into the ocean. Then it started. Up and down, up and down. They told me it was the ocean swell and as you looked out, you could see these great big troughs and we were heading straight for them. That was me finished - six more days in the cabin. Just imagine, twelve days on an ocean going liner and all I saw were the walls of my bloody cabin."

Ken also had the opportunity to visit Germany:

"I think a lot of it was to do with Bert. He'd done so well over here that City seemed to be the English club to be invited over for pre-season tours. I used to enjoy it, but I remember Bert getting one over on me in Düsseldorf. We went to the stadium to have a look at where we'd be playing and as we were walking round the pitch with our hosts, there was this laddie out on the pitch doing some ball work. Bloody hell, he was fantastic. His ball skills were really staggering and, don't forget, I'm saying this as a pro myself. I nudged Bert and he nodded at me, to tell me he'd seen him. I think he was pretty impressed as well. I started to think about the game and the possibility of coming up against this laddie. I was rather hoping he wasn't the inside-left. I told Bert to ask our German hosts what position this lad played. He turned round and spoke to them in German and they all started laughing. Bert turned to me and said the lad we were watching couldn't get in the team. I said this lot must be useful if he can't get in and Bert just laughed and explained. He said he can't get in because he's not a footballer, he's a juggler in a show in the town. It turned out he used to train at the football club to keep fit. I'm sure he'd have made a player though."

Towards the back end of Ken's time at Maine Road, City signed a player who did measure up to any footballing yardstick of greatness. When Denis Law arrived from Huddersfield Town in 1960, skipper Ken Barnes took the young Scot under his wing. They have remained friends ever since, and Ken still remembers the impact of the mercurial Law:

"Bloody hell! What a player he was! He didn't look much at first viewing. A skinny little bugger, he was. If I'm being honest - he looked like a stiff breeze would blow him over. Talk about appearances being deceptive. He was the perfect inside-forward. He could do everything. He was like lightning, he grafted, he could lick people, he scored goals - wonderful, absolutely top class. Of course, a lot of United supporters remember Denis as a striker, and he was, without a doubt, one of the best goalscorers ever. He was up there with anyone I've ever seen, and I've seen a few. But I always tell anyone who'll listen, that he had so much more to his game than just goals. As a youngster, he reminded me of Peter Doherty and I can't pay him a bigger compliment than that. A marvellous player, you couldn't take your eyes off him. Funnily enough, he could be a quiet laddie off the field, but on it, the bugger looked like he owned the bloody place. He had a bit of devil about him - no one took liberties with Denis. I suppose I kept an eye out for him, at first, because I was captain and he was a young lad and new to the club.

"We were also both practical jokers and wind up merchants. I always thought I could work a trick on someone, but, one time, I got caught out by Denis and the lads, in a way I'll never forget. The City lads were staying at a hotel in Eastbourne, ahead of a game in London on the Saturday. I wasn't with them, at first, because I was in Bristol, playing for the England 'B' team. I caught the train to Eastbourne on the Thursday and when I got there, all the lads were going on about this film they'd been to see the night before. The film was *Psycho* and they were talking about it, like it was the best film ever. In fairness to the lads, it wasn't just them, everyone was talking about it at the time.

"They kept telling me I really should go and see it and, of course, I fell for it. I said I'd go and see it that night and George Hannah said he'd come with me, because he fancied seeing it again. Anyway, we go off to the pictures, enjoy the film and then head back to the hotel. George was going on about the bit in the film with the old lady in the chair, and I must admit I had nearly jumped out of my skin at that part. When we got back, George went off to bed and I decided to have a bit of supper before heading for my room. When I got out of the lift a bit later, all the landing lights were out and when I got to my room, the door was ajar. As my eyes adjusted to the light, I looked into the room and saw what looked just like the little old lady from the bloody film, sat in a chair. Just as I'm edging my way in, I'm grabbed from behind and see this great big fuckin' knife whizzing past my head. I shit myself. It was Denis and the lads doing a "Psycho" on me. God, Denis had scared me half to death. I suppose it seems a bit childish now, but footballers the world over love wind-ups and he got me that night in Eastbourne, bloody hell he did.

"Despite the age difference, we've stayed friends over the years. I'd like to think I helped him to find his feet at Maine Road. Not so much on the park - he didn't need much help there - but as a young lad in a new city, maybe. I suppose it was like me arriving as a youngster 10 years earlier and striking up a friendship with Roy Paul, who was already a top international. Whatever the reason, me and Denis are still pals 40 odd years on, which can't be a bad thing."

As his time at Maine Road drew to a close, Ken, as ever, was happy to play without too much thought to the future:

"I never really considered what I would do when my time as a player was up - most players don't. You push it to the back of your mind, I suppose. It's a bit childish really, but it's like pretending it will go away if you don't think about it. When you've been lucky enough to play professional football, the last thing you want to think about is the time when it has to come to an end. In my case, I'd always been a bit casual about making plans, I was that type of person. At the back of my mind, I was like a lot of pros getting towards the back end of their playing days. Whatever the birth certificate may say, you always think there will be one more season in the old legs. We kid ourselves it will last forever."

If Ken was was not overly concerned with what the future might hold, others were already looking to him as a potential player-manager.

PART THREE

PASTURES NEW

Ken Barnes was approached by local businessmen, Peter Swales and Noel White, with a view to going to Altrincham as player-manager. They outlined their plans for the club and Ken could see the ambition and drive that would eventually take both men to the highest reaches of English football, but decided against a move to Moss Lane:

"I could see they wanted to get started in the game and had no doubt they had the desire to do what they said. I just felt though, that it was too big a drop from the first division to non-league. Looking back, I also think that, at the time, I was finding it difficult to see my future as anything but a player. Most footballers find it hard to think about not being players anymore."

When Ken found out that Wrexham were interested in him as a possible player-manager, he was in a quandary:

"Apparently, Matt Busby had recommended me, but I wasn't sure what the bloody hell to do. I'd never really thought about management. It's just the way I was really - enjoy my football and worry about tomorrow when it comes. The decision was down to me. City had offered me terms for another season, but nothing special.

"Wrexham were offering a pretty good deal (£22 per week!) and they were a league club, even if they were in the fourth division. City seemed happy enough for me to take the job, or at least they weren't begging me to stay or anything like that, but it was a real wrench to leave. I was in a right state as to whether I'd made the right decision or not. To be fair to City, they had been good to me. I'd had my 5-year loyalty bonus, £500 less tax, and my 10 year bonus, £750 less tax, so they had done okay by me - no question about it. In the end I decided to give it a go."

So Ken Barnes was now player-manager at the Racecourse Ground and after the agonising was over, it was time to get his feet wet:

"I just got cracking and learned as I went along. They didn't send you off on management courses back then. I knew how I wanted to play the game. The things I believed in were the things I'd always believed in. I decided to get them playing a bit of football. I got in Wynn Davies, who went on to have a great career, of course. I got Kevin Keelan from Joe Mercer at Aston Villa and then sold him on to Norwich. I loved working with the players and still loved playing myself, but the non-playing part of management was the bit I struggled with. Let me say right off the bat that we did fine out on the pitch. We were promoted in our first season and just missed out in the next. The crowds were up around the 14,000 mark.

"Things were going really well on the field. In fact, I got a job offer. I suppose they'd call it being head hunted these days. A club out in Denmark, Brondshoj FC, wrote to me and said they'd been following my progress at Wrexham with great interest and wanted to offer me the job of first team coach with them. I'd never heard of them but with a young family to think about, I decided it wasn't worth considering. But at least it suggested I was doing okay at the Racecourse.

"We had our moments. I can remember a couple of years into my time there, I think it was in 1963, certainly it was a very long cold winter, and we drew Liverpool in the FA Cup. The pitch was unplayable by modern standards, but Bill Shankly was desperate to get the game played. I can still hear his voice in my earhole:

'It'll take a stud, Ken, it'll take a stud. Let's get going.'

"Looking back, the conditions were likely to help us more than them, in terms of being a bit of a leveller. He was absolutely dead set on playing though. Maybe he was thinking about fixture pile ups and stuff, but I don't think so. I think that Shanks was just being Shanks. He just couldn't stand the thought of another Saturday without his fix of football. Now, Bill really was a man who lived for the game, he truly did.

"I decided I needed some help with the reserve side and the youngsters and someone told me that Ken Roberts was working in Wrexham. Ken had been a good player at Aston Villa, but had had to finish early through injury. Anyway, I found out he was working at a local store in Wrexham as a salesman and I decided to call in and see him. We had a chat, I liked him right off the bat and offered him a job. As I say, I brought Ken in to help with the youngsters and that worked out fine and we had some good times together. But I just wasn't cut out to deal with directors who knew nothing about the game, but thought they knew everything. I bit my lip for a while, but I knew that wouldn't last."

Last it most certainly did not. The uneasy relationship, between Ken and his board of directors, came to a head in his third season at the club:

"This one director was a farmer. He really thought he knew the game and he was always trying to tell me who to pick. It got to the point where it was really starting to get my goat. Something had to give and one day we went head to head."

Head to head barely does it justice. Ken was, and is, very frank in expressing his opinions, as the director was about to find out:

"'Look, you're a farmer right? Do I tell you how to milk a fuckin' cow? This is football and if I threw you a ball, you wouldn't know how to blow the fuckin' thing up!'

'We employ you!'

'Yes, you do - but you don't fuckin' own me.'"

Soon after, the farmer became the Chairman and Ken Barnes was sacked.

KEN ROBERTS

Ken Roberts played for Aston Villa in the 1950s, before being forced to finish prematurely with a damaged cruciate ligament in his knee. Still faced with the need to make a living, Ken returned to his native North Wales, where he worked in a furniture store. He was, of course, aware that Ken Barnes had joined Wrexham as player-manager but even so, he was still surprised to see the former City man striding across the store towards him one day. After a brief chat, Ken Barnes told his namesake to go and hand in his notice, he was going to work at Wrexham. Roberts did not have to agonise too long over his decision:

"Not for a second. The chance was there, to be back in the game with someone like Ken Barnes. It was a gift from Heaven, no question about it. I barely stopped to get my coat, I was that excited.

"I'd played against Ken for Aston Villa and I knew just how good a player he'd been and still was. Absolutely superb. I remember once playing against Manchester City and being told by my manager to 'pick up the number four'. Easier said than done, I can tell you. It was impossible to know what to do for the best. Time and again, we'd be bearing down on City's goal and, suddenly, Ken would turn and head for the halfway line. That wasn't what you expected from a right-half in the 50s. We're attacking and it's all looking very promising, so you'd expect their half back to be in there, with defensive duties the number one priority. So why was the right-half heading the other way? Next thing you know, Bert Trautmann's caught the cross or stopped the shot and he's looking to find Ken with a quick throw. All of a

sudden, we're the ones defending. It was unbelievable at times.

"Even at Wrexham, he might have been into his 30s, but he still had so much class. It's funny you know, but if you had to tell someone who'd never seen him, about Ken Barnes the footballer, they'd never believe you. It's a lot easier to tell people what he couldn't do. He certainly couldn't head or tackle. He wasn't a great striker of the ball and he could run around, but he wasn't quick. All these things he couldn't do, but if he was playing well, nobody could stop him passing you to death. We were 2-0 down to Barnsley in one game. Ken was really disappointed at half time. He looked round the dressing room and just said: 'We're the ones in red'. The point was made. His final instruction was for the lads to give him the ball every chance they got. Ken was magnificent in the second half and we won 6-2. He really was that good.

"I knew Ken the wonderful player, before I got to know Ken the man. When I did get to know him, well, all I can say is that I'd do anything for him. Don't get me wrong, Ken's no plaster saint. He's made mistakes and has his faults like the rest of us, but I'd trust him with my life, I really would.

"It was a magical time at the Racecourse. I think he should have been given more time, but I suppose, it was always going to be difficult for Ken. Being the manager means dealing with directors and Ken could never feel easy with the idea that someone who knew nothing about the game could tell him what to do and stick his nose into the football side of the club. It was great while it lasted though. Whatever problems Ken had with directors, he had an unbelievable ability to make the players feel ten feet tall.

"One of my favourite memories of Ken, back then, was one of his little pre-match ploys. He always dressed immaculately and on match days, he would sit just inside the door of the home dressing room at the Racecourse with a glass of whisky or sherry in his hand. The door would be wide open, so that Ken and the lads could see into the corridor as the visiting team arrived. When the opposition came in, they had to walk past the home dressing *room and the first thing they would see was Ken - dressed to the nines and without a care in the world - having a little glass of something, before getting changed. With perfect timing, Ken would break off his conversation with his own lads, look the visitors up and down, turn back and say:*

"'Look at these fuckin' donkeys. Nothing to beat again today, lads.'

"Then he'd kick the door shut. Superb stuff.

"Ken Barnes, for my money, has been a giant of the game. I've got the greatest respect for him as a player and as a man. Lots of people should be grateful for what Ken has done in the game. No one is more grateful than me, for the day I looked up and saw Ken walking towards me in a Wrexham furniture shop."

A USEFUL LITTLE SIDE

After leaving Wrexham, Ken was offered the job of player-manager at Rochdale, but decided against it. Although he still enjoyed playing and working with players, the others facets of management held very little interest for him:

"The game was changing but clubs were still, pretty much, run by directors who knew nothing about the game, but wanted to interfere anyway. Obviously, some managers were better than others at dealing with that sort of thing, but it wasn't for me. If I've got something to say, I say it, but back then you were supposed to sit back and listen if a director was talking - even if he was talking a load of bollocks. I'd tried it and knew I just couldn't do all the diplomatic stuff. If I'd taken the job, I would have been up against the same load of shit I'd had at the Racecourse. I'd have been kidding myself, to pretend things would have been different. If I'm honest, I was probably a little bit disillusioned with the game. I was certainly disheartened. I'd done a good football job at Wrexham but as for the rest of it, well, no thanks. In fact, Don Revie phoned me up and said that, if I wanted to get back into the game, he'd do everything he could to help me. It was a lovely offer from a good man, but I told him straight off that I needed a bit of breathing space, away from football."

With a young family, Ken still had to earn a living and with the help of former City director, Ian Niven, found himself working for a steel stockholder in Mossley:

"I really enjoyed it. I was out and about, pretty much my own boss. I won't deny that my time in football opened a few doors. I can remember calling into a factory out Liverpool way. I went inside and the receptionist phoned through, spoke to someone, put the phone down and told me the buyer was too busy to see me. That happened in that line of work, so I left my card with the receptionist, asked her if she'd be kind enough to pass it onto the buyer when she got the chance, thanked her and left. I was just getting into my car, when this chap came running up, puffing and blowing, and asked if I was Ken Barnes. I said yes, and he asked if I was Ken Barnes, the former City player. He was bloody delighted when I told him I was. He turned out to be a real football fan. I did some some great business with him after that. I got some bloody great orders from him. I don't kid myself that it was my great salesmanship, not a chance. Playing for City got me in there. I like to think I did a good job for him though. Football might have provided the opening, but I always tried to do a good job for my customers. I spent a fair bit of time talking about football as well as steel, though. As an icebreaker, there was nothing to touch it."

The enduring attraction of football was to exert its influence on Ken before too long :

"I met a chap called Tom Stelfox. He worked in insurance, but was also the Chairman of Witton Albion. We got talking and before I knew it, he'd offered me the chance to take over as player-manager at Wincham Park and he'd also offered me a day job, working in insurance. I'd had a break from the game by then, and, maybe, I'd had the chance to get the Wrexham experience out of my system. But I was ready to get back into the mix, I knew that much. It was a different level, but I was glad to be back. Funnily enough, I didn't really think I'd missed the game that much - till I got back into it. It's like a drug isn't it?

"It worked out alright. At that level, the politics weren't as bad. The directors couldn't swan about thinking they were God. I was getting on a bit, but could still do a job at Witton. I was reasonably happy with the day job and I was playing football the rest of the time. I'd done that before my days as a full-time professional, and enjoyed it, and it was the same now.

"We put a nice little side together. I got Chris Nicholl from Burnley on a free, and he went on to win the European Cup with Aston Villa and have a bloody great career there and at Southampton. Goalkeeper Peter Mellor came from City. Later on, he went back into the League and then got to play in the FA Cup Final with Fulham in the 1970s. I nearly got Tommy Booth on loan from City. I thought it was, more or less, sorted out and then, bugger me, within two weeks he's in City's first team and never came out again for years. What a signing that would have been. Anyone could see Tommy was destined to be a top player. Even so, it would have been great to have had someone of that quality turn out a few times for Witton Albion.

"Sadly, it didn't work out. But even without him, we were a tidy little outfit, not too bad at all. I also got Dennis Viollet and Bobby Johnstone to play for us. They were getting on a bit, of course, and their days at the top were over, just like mine, but at that level they could play with their heads and leave the running and chasing to the young kids. Can you imagine going to watch Witton Albion, nowadays, and seeing those two run out of the tunnel? Bloody hell, I think it must have been a thrill for the Witton fans, back then, to see those two playing for their club. It certainly excited me. Obviously, they were pals of mine, but anyone who has a love for the game, has got to want to see those two in the same side - even if they were puffing and blowing a bit.

"I seemed to be going along quite nicely, really. After my time in insurance, based in Manchester on Portland Street, I went back into the steel business and started working for Jack Walker, would you believe, and that was a good move for me. I was getting ready to move from Witton Albion to Bangor City and things seemed to be going pretty well. As I remember, I wasn't itching to get back into the pro game full-time, certainly not as a manager. But I've always been the same. If something suits me right now, I've never been one to think too much about what my next move will be. Of course, I felt I had something to offer, after my time at the highest level, but I didn't spend hours scheming how to get back in. Funnily enough though, even if I don't remember chomping at the bit to be back in League football, I didn't have to think twice when Joe Mercer asked me to go back to Manchester City. Maybe, it was a more a case of not letting myself think about it. I'm pretty good at just enjoying the moment. It's the story of my life, really."

As ever with Ken, long term plans didn't really come into the equation. But, with his former side reaching the heights under Joe Mercer and Malcolm Allison, a career back in big time football was about to beckon.

PART FOUR

BACK TO THE BLUES

Ken Barnes admits that his return to Maine Road owed little to strategy: "Oh good God no! It must have been fate, because I certainly didn't plan it. I bumped into Joe Mercer at a social event. He was always nice to me and always seemed to show me a bit of respect. I'm never quite sure why he took to me. He always said I'd extended his playing career by 10 years, because a lot of the press referred to me as the new Joe Mercer. I suppose we were similar in playing style and with us both being skinny and bandy as well, you could see where the comparison came from.

"Anyway, we got talking and at that time, of course, City were bloody flying. I'd just left Witton to go to Bangor City, so I couldn't believe it when he asked me if I wanted to go back to Maine Road as reserve team manager. He said the job was mine, if I wanted it. Did I want it! I've often wondered why he offered the job to me. We were acquaintances rather than friends, though I always found him easy to talk to whenever I did bump into him. But if you think about it, at that time, Manchester City were the most successful club in the country. Most people in the game would have jumped at the chance to be involved with them. Maybe Joe was aware of what I'd done at Wrexham and Witton. I'll never know now, of course. Whatever it was that prompted him to ask me, I'm bloody glad he did. It mapped out my life for the next 30 years.

"He said he'd be in touch. A few days later, I got a call from Joe sounding a bit embarrassed. He asked me if I'd apply in writing for the job. I said: 'Joe, you've already offered me the job'. He said: 'Yes Ken, but it has to go through the proper channels, apparently.' Well, I let him have it: 'Fuckin' hell, Joe, are you a man or a mouse?' I really thought that in his position, after all he'd achieved, he should have just told the board what he was going to do and then just done it. You can't imagine Alex Ferguson coming back to tell me to apply in writing can you? Anyway, I did apply and it all went through without a hitch."

After nearly a decade away, Ken Barnes was back at Manchester City and pleased to be there:

"It was unbelievable to be back at Maine Road. In some ways it was just the same, but when I'd left, the side was going downhill. Now, the place was bloody buzzing. They had some marvellous players in the first team and I had some good youngsters in the reserves. I wasn't bothered, in the slightest, about not being the manager. I'd learnt at Wrexham, that the politics of football just wasn't me at all. I was a tracksuit man at heart; looking to help the kids develop. Not coaching as such - just a bit of help and advice along the way.

"You couldn't help watching and getting excited about some of the talent at the club though. Bloody hell you couldn't. As I said before, when I'd left they were on the slide, and now, less than 10 years later, they had some exceptional players.

"I thought Colin Bell was a tremendous all round pro and a real player's player. I really couldn't find fault with him. A magnificent athlete, of course, but so much more than that. If there's never been a perfect player, Colin got a lot closer than most, there's no doubt about that. Top class, sheer quality - as good as you'll ever see.

"Mike Summerbee, what a winger! Pace, tenacity, a great crosser of the ball and that bit of devil you don't always expect in a wideman. He could also play centre-forward because he had the ability to hold the ball up so well. He was the most tenacious winger I ever saw. Nobody took liberties with Mike, nobody.

"Franny Lee was a bit like Mike, in many respects. He never ducked out, had great feet, he was stocky and powerful and he could skin people. He could have played anywhere, Franny. A real bundle of energy and talent.

"I loved Neil Young as a player. He was so elegant and had so much talent, plus a cracking left foot. I think that, maybe, he was a bit underestimated by some of the fans sometimes. But for me, he had real quality. A real class act.

"Tony Coleman came in and did a reasonable job. Without being too hard on the lad, he was in the right place at the right time. Off the pitch, and sometimes on it, he was a bit wild. To be honest, I thought he was a bit barmy, really.

"Alan Oakes was a real powerhouse. So consistent, so hard working. He wasn't the greatest creatively, but a real team man. He might not win too many man of the match awards, but you had to watch a lot of football to see him have a bad game.

"Tony Book must have thought he was living out his dreams at City, starting as late as he did. He was a good defender with real pace. Tony had terrific application. He got his chance, at the top level of the game, at an age when a lot of players would already have finished and then won more medals than most footballers could dream of. That tells its own story.

"I also thought Tommy Booth was a genuine football talent. Not a great tackler, really, he preferred to nick the ball away rather than clatter someone. But he had great anticipation and real football savvy and he could play it out from the back. Yes, Tommy Booth really was a fine footballer.

"Mike Doyle was a bit of a mystery to me. Don't get me wrong, he had a very good career and certainly made the most of the talent he'd been given, no question about it. But I could never quite square up his hard man image, with the way he used to go down so easily. In fact, when I was the trainer and it was my job to run on to treat injuries and such like, I never used to bother for Mike, unless the referee shouted me on. I sometimes thought he went down so much because he liked to hear the crowd cheer when he got back up!

"Glynn Pardoe was a good full back. Funnily enough, he was playing as a forward when I first saw him. I was at Wrexham at the time. I didn't think too much of him up front, to be honest, but when he moved back, well, he was fine. He had good control and could pass a good ball and, although he looked quite solid, he had a bit of pace about him."

Ken was in his element working back at City. However, he soon became aware that the brilliant alliance between Joe Mercer and Malcolm Allison, that had taken the club to the pinnacle of the English game, was starting to pull apart: "Joe and Malcolm had achieved unbelievable success as a pairing. They were like chalk and cheese, really. Joe was an absolute gentleman. A top class chap, no doubt about. He was very down to earth and worked hard to build up a real spirit in the club. He had been a very fine player, of course. He was old school, in as much as he was more concerned about the quality of the players than about systems. He must have seen something in Malcolm and his ideas that sparked his interest, though.

"Malcolm was always full of new ideas and wanting to try things and Joe was the older, more experienced head, a calming influence in many ways. It was never dull around Malcolm. Sometimes, he disappeared up his own arsehole with his theories, but Joe was there to rein him in if he went a bit too far. It had worked brilliantly for City so far, but it only took five minutes to see it was a relationship under strain. I was finding my feet and concentrating on my own job, but anyone at the club could see what was happening. Malcolm wanted to be the manager, no question about it. He wanted recognition of his contribution to the team's success. My first impression of him was that success had gone to his head a bit. He had a bit of swagger, a bit of swank about him. I remember, I was out with him once and a fan shouted over, 'Hiya Malcolm, how's Joe?'

Malcolm shouted back: 'Joe who? I run the team'.

I thought to myself: 'You big-headed ****'".

The power struggle continued, with Joe Mercer reluctant to accept a move 'upstairs', to the position of general manager: "Joe still thought of himself as close to the players. He wanted the day to day involvement, not to be stuck in an office. I think he felt a bit betrayed by Malcolm, while Malcolm was convinced it was time for him to be given the reins. I told Joe to stay and work it out. After all, look at what they'd done for the club together."

In October 1971, Joe Mercer became general manager, with Malcolm Allison now the team manager. By March 1972, the Blues looked well on course for the League title, when Malcolm paid £200, 000 to Queens Park Rangers for Rodney Marsh. If Marsh was intended to be the final piece in the title jigsaw, the plan went sadly awry and City missed out by a point. Even now, well over 30 years later, the argument continues as to the merits of the flamboyant Marsh. Ken Barnes was not a great fan:

"Rodney Marsh was not a great player, no way. To be fair to him, he had a bit of talent on the ball, but without the vision to harness it for the good of the team. He was what we used to call a tuppenny ha'penny ball player - very skilful, but very little end product."

By the end of April, the title had gone. By the end of June, so had Joe Mercer:

"When he told me he was off to Coventry City as general manager, I was stunned. If he wasn't happy to be general manager at Maine Road, why would he want to go to Highfield bloody Road? For the life of me, I just couldn't see the sense in it."

Once Joe had gone, Malcolm asked Ken to help out with the first team:

"I don't know why he asked me, because he never listened to anything I had to say. We never really got close. We were very different, in all fairness. Can you imagine? My views on coaching and I'm 'assisting' the game's number one coaching guru? I don't bloody think so. For all his qualities, Malcolm couldn't or wouldn't accept that he was better in combination with Joe than he was on his own. Perhaps it was pride, or ego or both. He didn't last long after Joe went. Let's be honest - he made a right balls of it. A few years later, they had a do for Malcolm and his son had a bit of a go at me, for not acknowledging what Malcolm had done in his career as a manager. I told him straight: 'Malcolm as a coach - first class, as a manager, no fuckin' way!'"

By March 1973, Malcolm Allison had moved onto Crystal Palace and the Mercer - Allison years at Manchester City were over.

COLIN BELL

Any poll of Manchester City fans, asked to name the best post-war player for the club, would end, almost certainly, in a landslide victory for Colin Bell. He was an awe-inspiring mixture of phenomenal athleticism and football excellence. Ken Barnes makes this assessment of a truly great player:

"I don't suppose there's ever been a complete player, but Colin Bell got closer than most. He had just about every quality you would look for in a truly great player."

Colin has no memories of Ken Barnes the player and was an established international by the time Ken returned to Maine Road under Joe Mercer. According to Ken, he returned to Maine Road as reserve team manager, but Colin remembers it somewhat differently:

"Ken was part of the management team, but it seemed to the

players that it was quite a fluid set up. Ken always seemed to be part of whatever was going on at the club. He had a bit of a floating role, I suppose you'd say. I even remember him running on with the magic sponge occasionally. I'm sure he never had any qualifications as a physio, as he'd need to have nowadays. It wouldn't have mattered anyway. With Ken, it was the sponge or nothing. In fact, I can remember Mike Doyle going down in a game at Maine Road, when Ken was on the sponge. Ken didn't move at first - he always thought Doyley went down a bit too easily. In the end, the referee had to order him onto the field to do the necessary. Well, Ken had to run 60 or 70 yards to treat him. Mike was lying there groaning and Ken was asking him what the problem was:

'Is it a twist? Have you pulled a muscle?'

'Ken, it's my ca. . . , it's my ca. . . "

"It's your what, for fuck's sake? Your calf?"

"No Ken, It's my catarrh.'

Well, Ken went ballistic:

*'Catarrh? Fuckin' catarrh? I've run 70 fuckin' yards because you've got catarrh? Get up, you big soft ****!'*

Then Ken ran off and left Mike to his own devices. Priceless, but typical Ken."

After Colin Bell's career came to a premature conclusion through injury, he had little connection with Maine Road for a number of years. It was largely through Ken that he was drawn back into the fold:

"Apart from my family, football had been my life, but I never wanted to be a manager. I'm a shy person, really, and I don't like the limelight, but when I got out of the restaurant business, at the end of the 1980s, I found myself spending time in Ken's office at Maine Road. It was wonderful. Whatever time you called in you would find Ken and anything up to a dozen ex-players talking about football and putting the game to rights. You never knew who you'd bump into, though Denis Law was a regular, as I recall.

As soon as you arrived, Ken would sort out a pot of tea and before you knew it, you were talking football and listening to Ken and his stories. It was a great place for someone like me. I could talk about the game, amongst my peers, with no pressure. I started to be a regular and Ken was obviously listening and watching.

"One day, he took me to one side and asked me if I fancied joining the scouting staff, working with the kids. He told me there wasn't much money in it, but I wasn't bothered about that. It was perfect for me. Can you imagine how it felt for me? After all those years away, Ken Barnes thought I had something to offer to Manchester City. I was thrilled, really thrilled. I was working for the club I loved, in a role I enjoyed. I loved my time there and I really thrived in the job. Being a shy person myself, I suppose I understood just how difficult it could be for the younger lads trying to find their feet. I always gave them a chance. Or if they froze when they came to Maine Road, I'd go and take another look.

"Ken had a great set up there and don't be fooled; it's not easy to judge youngsters, but his record speaks for itself. Absolutely phenomenal. The kids loved him, but they also respected him. He was a player's man and they knew that.

"As a bloke, Ken is just great, I love him. Straight, blunt even, but dead honest. He always believed that the players were the most important part of the club and he wasn't afraid to let the directors know it. That was Ken.

"When it comes to coaching, you know what Ken's like. I must say, my own ideas are pretty close to his. Out on the pitch, I always felt it was my job to give 100% concentration for every minute of the game. I didn't think it was down to someone on the touchline to tell me what to do. I've got a coaching badge somewhere, but I can't remember what they asked me and I'm not sure if I'd pass it now.

"Ken Barnes might not think much of coaching badges, but I'll tell you something. If they handed out badges for smoking,

drinking and swearing, he'd have an office full!"

MIKE SUMMERBEE

Mike Summerbee was part of the great Manchester City side of the late 60s and is still involved with the commercial side of his beloved Blues. An international player who became an all-time favourite with City fans, he possessed a fire and "tenacity" (Ken's description) that you do not readily associate with widemen.

His first memories of Ken Barnes, go back to his time as a young fan: *"We lived in Cheltenham and I used to catch the train up to Birmingham, to watch football. Birmingham City, Aston Villa and West Bromwich Albion were all in the old first division, so that one hour train ride meant I had my pick and I could go wherever I wanted in Birmingham to see my favourite players. Ken was a magnificent player, absolute quality, with an unbelievable football brain. I can still see him now. City would be defending and as soon as a cross went into their box and Ken knew Bert Trautmann was going to get it, he'd be heading the other way, waiting for Bert's clearance and looking to get something going forward. He always wanted to be setting up attacking moves. Funnily enough, one of my other favourites was another wing-half at West Brom called Ray Barlow. He may have possibly won one cap for England. To think that Ray and Ken didn't win a stack of England caps between them was scandalous really. I never got the chance to play with or against Ken in a competitive game, but I do remember when he was player-manager at Wrexham and I played there with Swindon. He wasn't playing that day, but he gave me plenty of verbals from the dug-out. When Joe Mercer brought Ken back to City, I'd been at Maine Road a while and I'd done okay in the game, but I was still in awe of him. I still had my boyhood memories of him as a great player.*

"Over the years, we've become great friends and with Ken, what you see is what you get. He tells it to you straight but when he talks about football you listen, because he knows this game inside out. I think every one of us had a great respect for him. He had a way with him. It's hard to explain but if Ken said even a few words to you, somehow it registered and stuck with you. For example, you might get a bit of a bollocking about something at half time and you'd be walking back out down the tunnel for the second half. He'd just have a little word. Nothing major, but somehow it always seemed to pick you up and make you want to get out there and prove yourself. His words carried weight, because you knew he'd been there, done it and bought the t- shirt.

"As you know, Ken has his very strong views on the merits of coaching. I don't totally agree with him on everything, because if you have the talent I think coaching can help you get the most from that talent. I do agree with him, though, that you have to have the gift in the first place. Football is basically a simple game but the ability to play it well, at the top level, is something you're born with, not taught.

"As for Ken's ability as a scout, what can you say? Look at his track record. Amazing. Ultimately, it must stem from his fantastic knowledge of the game. We all like to think we can spot a player, but with Ken it's like another sense. He can watch youngsters play and everyone will be raving about some kid who has caught the eye. But Ken will have seen something that will draw him to another youngster - a little piece of skill or whatever. Somehow, but don't ask me exactly how because I don't know, he can tell the kids who have that bit of something to go on to the next level from those who look good now but are never going to go higher. If you look at the list of players he brought to Maine Road you can't really overstate what he has done for the club.

"Ken Barnes is a true football man. I was in awe of him as a kid and I'm proud to call him my friend now. I had a wonderful time as a player at City and I'm lucky that people still talk about the *side I played in, more than 30 years after our heyday. People talk about us and you hear the word "legend" sometimes. It's nice, of course it is, but I'm telling you, Ken Barnes is a real football legend."*

FRANCIS LEE

Francis Lee enjoyed a football career of the highest order with Bolton Wanderers, Manchester City, Derby County and England and returned to Maine Road, as Chairman, in the early 90s. Over the years, he has developed a close friendship with Ken Barnes and it's an association that goes back to Lee's first team debut for Bolton:

"*I made my debut at Burnden Park, aged 16, against Manchester City and Ken Barnes was playing for them. I scored after just 15 minutes with a header against Bert Trautmann. It was unbelievable really. But Ken was a smashing player, he really was. He wasn't a hard tackling, grafting wing-half - he was a real football purist. He believed, and still does believe, that the game should be about skill and craft, not just sweat. He had a fantastic eye for a pass, very astute. He certainly wasn't the best defensively, but if the radar was working he could thread passes through you, that other players wouldn't even have dreamt of. He really did have lovely skill on the ball.*

"*Funnily enough, I always liked to watch Ken take penalties. I took a few myself, over the years and I had the reputation for giving the ball a good crack. Ken took a penalty like he did everything else in the game - with the emphasis on craft. He liked to deceive the keeper into going the wrong way and then he'd just nurse the ball into the opposite corner. Typical Ken. Mind you, if the goalie did guess right, he had to walk forward out of his goal to pick the ball up!*

"*Over the years, Ken and I have spent untold hours talking* about the game. He can be very dogmatic. You won't shift him from his beliefs about the game, especially when it comes to coaching. To a large extent I agree with him. Good players win you matches, not coaches. When I hear coaches talking about shaping a side, I always have to smile. The shape of a football team is dictated by the brains of the best players. We've had a few discussions about wingers over the years. We've argued about the demise of the winger, and I told Ken straight that when I started, the easiest thing was to get the ball and the hardest thing was to do something with it. With the advent of the back four, that was stood on its head. For a wideman now, the hardest thing is to get the ball, the easiest, is to do something with it once you've got it.

"Ken loves to talk about the game. His office at Maine Road was famous as a place to find football people putting the world to rights. You had to wait for the smoke to clear to see who was in there, though.

"Ken is one of the straightest talkers you'll ever meet. Ask him a question and you will always get an honest answer. Like it or lump it. He'd never have made a diplomat, but you always knew where you stood with him. He's a real football man and footballers recognise that. Senior pros or the kids he signed, they all loved him.

"When he came back to City under Joe Mercer he did every job going. I was never quite sure what his title was at any given time. The thing about Ken was he was always there and always involved. He liked a laugh and a joke and he could take it as well as give it. I remember Malcolm taking us all off to the Norbreck Castle Hotel in Blackpool. Ken was with us, as usual. One morning we went out for a run and we ran miles into the teeth of a freezing wind, blasting in from the Irish Sea. It was murder, it really was, till we turned back for home. With the wind at our backs, well, we just bowled along. Footballers being footballers, someone had to pay for making us run. Just at that moment, who comes along, puffing and blowing, but Ken Barnes. We were on the beach and the tide had not been out long and there were great pools of icy cold seawater everywhere. Well, we grabbed Ken, stripped him off and carried him to one of the pools. He was fighting like mad, his back was arching and his false teeth were hanging out. In he went and off we went. We left him with just an old trainer's jersey to cover his modesty. He had to run back to the hotel, over the prom, holding the jersey down to cover his assets and then ask at reception for his key.

"Another time we were on tour in Greece and we were lazing around the pool when Ken appeared looking like a bottle of sterilised milk in swimming trunks. I've never seen anything so white in my life. He asked if anyone had any sun tan oil. Well, Rodney Marsh just chucked him a bottle and told him to try it. Ken just slapped it on, a bit here, a bit there and sprawled on a sunbed. Rodney showed me the bottle and it wasn't sun tan oil. It was that fake tan cream and, I can tell you, it wasn't very sophisticated stuff back in the 70s. When Ken stood up, 15 minutes later, he looked like Chief Sitting Bull!

"There were always lots of laughs to be had, whenever Ken was around but joking apart, his contribution to the club was massive. The kids he signed, well what can you say? He had a terrific eye for a player and he cared about his kids and they knew it and respected him for it. Ken's one of the all time greats. God bless him. I'm proud to know him."

FOLLOW THAT

If the departure of Malcolm Allison marked the end of an era for Manchester City, the immediate priority for the club was to appoint a successor. Chairman Peter Swales asked Ken Barnes to be caretaker manager at Maine Road, but Ken said no:

"I was tempted, of course I was, because we're talking about managing Manchester City for goodness sake. But whatever the temptation, deep down, I knew I couldn't work with Peter Swales. You want to help but you have to be realistic. The pull of the club is very powerful but I think I'd reached an age when you know a bit more about yourself and what will work and what won't work. Peter Swales and Ken Barnes? Not a fuckin' chance."

The post went to Johnny Hart, a former player who had moved onto the coaching staff. Ken was to be his right-hand man:

"It was never going to be easy for Johnny. He was a good lad, who'd been a good player. He was a bit laid back, like, but I thought he knew enough about the game to make a good job of it. But don't forget, he was taking on an ageing team that had done wonders and that makes it really hard when the time comes to change things. How do you tell a player, who's been part of all that success, that his days are numbered? Don't get me wrong, it was still a good team, but things would need changing sooner rather than later. Johnny had problems with his health and there were elements of the job that he just couldn't cope with. He found it really difficult to drop players or even leave them out, if they told him they should be in team. I remember telling him straight: 'Fuckin' Hell Johnny, we've all been left out at sometime or other and every player thinks he should be in the bloody team - that's why they're players.'

"Looking back, maybe Johnny took on the job out of a sense of duty to the club, without thinking it through. Maybe he let his loyalty and sense of pride rule his head. It's a shame, because I'm sure he was desperately keen to do well for City. He was a former player, after all, and loved the place. It just proved too much for him - he was gone in a few months.

"There is one thing Johnny will be remembered for I'm sure. On my recommendation, he brought Denis Law back to Maine Road. I knew Denis was getting on a bit, but I also knew what he had left to give. Especially with his pride hurt, that United would let him go and let him go to us, of all places. Alright, he'd had his problems with injury and most of his career was definitely behind him, but I'd known him a long time. He wasn't the player he had been, but make no mistake; Denis Law was top quality and even three-quarters of the old Denis was well worth having. Even past his best I felt that he would rise to one more challenge and I was right. I suppose that, more than anything, the City fans remember his second spell with the Blues for that goal at Old Trafford. But I was just pleased to see Denis back with that old swagger. He's a bright lad, he knew it was his swansong, but it was great to see him enjoy that swansong in a City shirt."

When Johnny Hart resigned on the grounds of ill heath, Peter Swales again offered the job, as caretaker, to Ken Barnes. Once again Ken declined: "Same reason as before. I'd have fallen into the same trap as Johnny Hart, if I'd let my heart rule my head."

For a replacement, Peter Swales looked outside the club and that signalled the arrival of Ron Saunders from Norwich City.

THE SERGEANT-MAJOR

Ron Saunders arrived from Norwich with a reputation as a disciplinarian and seemed determined to impose himself on a dressing room packed with stars. Coming to Manchester City represented a major step up for Saunders. Ken Barnes' first impression was of a man intent on showing everyone who was boss: "Let's have it right, it was never likely to be easy for Ron Saunders. He'd done well at a small club but it was a bloody big step up for him to take over at Maine Road. He must have thought of how he was going to impose himself on a group of players who had been right at the top of their profession for years, and he chose to do it a certain way.

"It doesn't look too wise a choice looking back, but then hindsight is a wonderful thing. That said, in football, as in any walk of life, respect is something you earn rather than demand. He was very abrupt and, right from the off, he had a very confrontational relationship with the senior players. He called them "old men" and organised training matches between them and the youngsters. I suppose he was trying to make the point that reputations counted for nothing, only what happened on the pitch. But it seemed like he was belittling them and their achievements for the club. It's a long way back from there. Nobody and nothing lasts forever, of course it doesn't, but recognising that it's time to move on is one thing, appearing to mock previous glories, and the men who'd shared them, is something else altogether.

"He had a manner that got a few backs up, including mine. It may have been bravado, of course. A new man in the biggest job of his life and working with some of the best players in the country, all of whom had been at the club for ages. He may have been covering up nerves or something. Whatever the reason, he was very abrasive. One day, we were doing some shooting practice and at the end he turned to me and told me to collect the balls. It was like he was talking to a fuckin' apprentice. That was it, I blew my top.

'Collect the fuckin' balls! I'm not the fuckin' ball boy!'"

Shortly afterwards, Saunders moved Ken to chief scout, following the retirement of the legendary Harry Godwin. Ken was not overly bothered. In fact, he was about to embark on a phase of his career, that would never lose its fascination:

"I was happy to get out of coaching. They were bringing in psychologists and bleedin' ballet dancers! Not my cup of tea at all. The coaching culture was going mad and I'd never been a fan. I'd gone on a course taken by Walter Winterbottom once. Turgid, pedantic stuff. There was a course book as I recall. Fuck me! Read the book, pass the course. No thanks. I could definitely see which way the wind was blowing. All the talk was about coaches. I remember thinking to myself; what about the fuckin' players? When I thought back to being a kid, I went to Birmingham or the Villa to see players. I could tell you the names of all the players, but could I tell you who the manager was? Could I balls. When I thought about my own playing days, it was always players I was thinking about. It seemed obvious to me, that football was about the lads out on the pitch but now everyone was on about bloody coaches.

"Anyway, scouting, be it recruiting kids or looking for senior pros - and I got to do plenty of both over the following 20-odd years - was something I was to find endlessly fascinating. I don't remember being daunted at following Harry. He was a great bloke with a deserved reputation as a top scout. I think we, probably, had a lot of beliefs in common, about how the job should be done. Remember, the scout is usually the first formal contact with a club for a boy and his parents. Their first impression of the club at a personal level. What is it they say? You never get a second chance to make a first impression.

"I was really lucky to have a great scouting partner in John Doherty, but the job of unearthing a true talent is a real challenge. Not only that, but I've always believed that life is there to be enjoyed and with John, there were always going to be a few laughs along the way. I've signed some good ones, and a couple of exceptional ones, over the years, and, as John will no doubt tell you, I've missed out on a few as well. But I've never lost the buzz you get when you spot a laddie who's got that little bit of something that tells you he's got a chance as a player."

As for Ron Saunders, he brought Dennis Tueart to Maine Road and took the team to the League Cup Final against Wolves in 1974. Sadly City lost 2-1, despite dominating the game, and as the club hovered above the danger zone in the league, Chairman Peter Swales decided that a change was needed. Saunders was sacked. Ken was not too surprised to see him go:

"Not really, no. He came to City and decided to get rid of the old guard. Maybe it needed to be done, it was certainly coming sooner rather than later. But he made it into a confrontation with a set of senior pros, who had a lot to be proud of from their time at Maine Road. His thinking may have been right, but his manner of doing things made it into a battle of wills. You have to remember where he was coming from. He was the new kid from a small town club, facing off against a bunch of players, who had earned their spurs with the supporters. Look at what they'd won, for Christ's sake. Whatever changes you believe need to be made, surely you still have to acknowledge the previous achievements, as part of the process of moving on. Otherwise, it looks as if you're dismissing what those players had done for the club. If you think about it, it's as much about manners as it is about management, I suppose. There was a lot of talk of "player power" at the time and there was some truth in that. It's one of the hardest jobs in football, to bite the bullet and recognise a team has reached the end of the line. But how he went about it, well, what can you say? Once he lost the players, the only defence was results and he didn't get those. It might have been different, if they'd won the League Cup."

Peter Swales decided to look inside the club for a new manager. Step forward Tony Book.

JOHN DOHERTY

Former Manchester United player, John Doherty, has known Ken Barnes since the early 50s. Along with a friendship that has endured for more than half a century, they were also scouting partners at Manchester City for many years. They hold many

ABOVE: *Ken's first trophy and the East Birmingham Shield*
(Ken is sat between the teachers)

BELOW: *RAF Stafford - Ken in service of King and Country*

*Ken Barnes
- the stylish wing-half*

Putting on the style

THE 1955 FA CUP FINAL: *always a struggle once Jimmy Meadows got injured'.
Here, Newcastle retake the news via Bobby Mitchell against ten-man City.*

*Ken with Bobby Johnstone, "on his day the
best I ever played with"*

Training with old pals Don Revie and Johnny Williamson

THE 1956 FA CUP LINE-UP: *the photo before the serious one (the groundsman has just turned on the sprinkler system behind the photographers' backs)*

BERT TRAUTMANNN GRABS THE BALL IN THE 1956 FINAL
'if there's ever been a better 'keeper, I've never seen him'

Roy Paul with a little help from Ken, Don Revie and Dave Ewing

'Time to relax and savour the occasion'

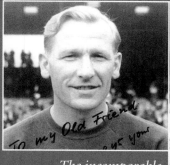

*The incomparable
Bert Trautmann*

Top: *Captain Ken alongside Denis Law described by Ken as a
'truly great player by any yardstick'.*

Below: *Ken and his 'very useful'
Wrexham team.*

Ken with City manager Tony Book following his return to the club.

Ken in his office - a sanctuary for footballers young and old.

KEN WITH SON PETER: *'Two generations of football excellence'*

Ken with Denis Law and Dennis Viollet,
'try buying those three if they were still 25'.

Ken with
John Doherty,
'The Manchester
Mafia'.

'Mr Barnes' and some
of his successful
recruits including Steve
Lomas, Paul Lake and
David White.

Ken in Malaysia 'still got it'.

Ken with a pachyderm City fan

Ken and the crown prince

*The 'mellow' Ken?
'Tell him Beckham is better
than Finney - see how mellow
he is then!'* JOHN BOND

footballing beliefs in common and when John Bond came from Norwich City, to take over as manager at Maine Road, he dubbed the pair the "Manchester Mafia". Bond grew to appreciate the knowledge and talent of the two and when he moved to Burnley, he recruited Doherty as his chief scout. Ken and John first met in a coffee bar near Deansgate in Manchester:

"I remember it well. It was the early 50s and Ken was ready to pack up and go home. He was so fed up with things at City, he really was ready to head back to Birmingham. Manchester City fans must be glad he didn't. What he did for them as a player and as a scout is unbelievable, really. Ken's name should be up in lights at the club. We've been friends ever since."

What did John Doherty, the scout, make of Ken Barnes the player?:

"He couldn't head, he couldn't tackle. He could run, but he had no pace and no left side to speak of - a fantastic player. With Ken, it was all between his ears. He had more than vision, he had imagination. I would love to have seen him play at the very highest level. I am absolutely convinced he would have been a great international player. Bad players can play with anyone, but good players need other good players around them - the higher they go, the better they get. Ken would have been in his element playing with footballers of international calibre. If you look at the players who got picked ahead of him for England, it's a joke. Back in the days of the selection committee, do you think it's a coincidence that Wolves had four half-backs play for England and their chairman was on the committee? Some of the players who were capped ahead of Ken, dear me. Well I still can't believe it nearly 50 years later."

In later life, John was Ken's scouting partner. Together, they travelled all over Britain, and beyond, looking for talent for Manchester City:

"I couldn't tell you the number of games we watched and the

players we recommended over the years. If you look at the talent Ken signed or recommended it must have saved City millions and that's just the ones who played for the first team. Don't forget all the lads he signed, who City got rid of or who went on to play at other clubs. We looked at players and I used to help out if there was a bit of negotiating to be done. You always think about the ones that got away, of course. We were watching a game at Atherstone and saw a striker we both liked the look of very much. We knew the other clubs would be sniffing, once they found out about him. We were desperate to get in to see the chairman of Atherstone after the game. We were just deciding how to get in to see him, when someone called my name. I couldn't believe it. It was a lad I'd played football with in Wythenshawe years ago. Turned out he was the groundsman at Atherstone. I asked him to get us in to see the chairman. He did, and we settled on fourteen thousand for the lad. We shot off back to Manchester and told Tony Book the good news. I still remember the look on Ken's face, when Bookie said he'd have to clear it with the Chairman: 'For fuck's sake Tony, he's going all the way to the top and he's ours for fourteen grand. Don't ask the Chairman, tell him you're signing the lad.'

"Tony Book refused to act without clearance. Two days later, that young striker signed for Leicester City for fourteen thousand pounds. He would go on to play for Arsenal and England. City had missed out on Alan Smith."

There is not a club in football, of course, that does not have such 'one that got away' tales. But even more than missing out on Alan Smith, John remembers his and Ken's efforts to get City to take a chance on a young goalscorer at Chester:

"Ken gave me a call and asked me to go with him to Chester. Alan Oakes, the former City midfielder, was the manager and had tipped Ken off about a teenage frontman he thought was real quality. We went over to have a look. The lad came on as sub and, straight off, it was obvious he was going places. After the

game, we went to see Alan and the Chairman and it was no secret that Chester were desperate for cash. We went back and told City that Chester wanted £50,000 for the youngster, but we thought it would be money well spent. We heard nothing, though we were told that Malcolm Allison had gone to see him a couple of times and couldn't decide it if was worth pursuing. In the meantime, Liverpool had decided that it was most definitely worth pursuing and had signed the kid. I think it's safe to say they got their 50 grand's worth out of Ian Rush."

Along with the highs and the lows of scouting, there were a few laughs along the way:

"For me and Ken watching football was a job, but a job to be enjoyed. I remember once we were at Halifax in the middle of winter, to look at a full back who'd been recommended to Ken. We battled our way there through the weather and sat down just as the players were coming out. The full back in question ran out and Ken turned to me and said,

'Seen enough, John?'

'Certainly have, Ken' I replied.

"The lad was knock-kneed and you don't find many good knock-kneed footballers. We were back in the car before they kicked off."

Ken Barnes had a phenomenal track record for signing youngsters, often in the face of the fiercest of competition from other, apparently more attractive clubs. John Doherty has the greatest admiration for what Ken achieved:

"They should have named City's academy after Ken. It'll have to run for years to produce a fraction of the talent Ken did. I'm sure you know about Ken's belief that the kids should see Maine Road as a special place and I'm positive that that was very important in bringing lads to the club. I'm sure there were a lot of elements that went together to do what he did but, for me, one of the most important things about Ken and the kids, was his approach to their talent. He always looked at a youngster and saw what he

could do, rather than what he couldn't. So many young lads get
their confidence battered by people telling them what they're not
good at. If a youngster went to Ken, or "Mister Barnes" as they all
called him, he would always pick them up and dust them off, by
reminding them that they wouldn't be here if they couldn't play.
I always thought that he had a wonderful rapport with the kids.
Ask any of them, I'm sure they'll tell you.

"Maybe, when someone has been part of a club for as long as
Ken was at City, people don't really see what an asset they have.
It's too close to home to appreciate. When Peter Reid got rid of
Ken, they came up with a pension that was a joke. If they'd stood
back and looked at what he had actually done, they should have
given him half a million quid at least."

Elsewhere in this book Ken Barnes admits, that towards the
end of his long scouting career, he was starting to get
discouraged by the dearth of talent. John Doherty can confirm
Ken's increasing disillusionment:

"We were sat in the stand, somewhere in the back of beyond. It
was obvious, after about five minutes, that there was nothing to
interest us out on the park. That seemed to be happening more
and more and Ken turned to me and said, 'I think we've seen
the best of it John. We're not going to find another Matthews or
Finney; those days are gone.'"

John Doherty and Ken Barnes have shared over 50 years as
friends and colleagues. Half a century is a long time, in life and
football. The game may have changed beyond all recognition,
but John is adamant that two things have not changed in that
time and never will change; Ken himself and his view of how
football should be played:

"Ken is Ken. People either love him or hate him. He has his
faults, and plenty of them, just like the rest of us, but he is the
same with everyone. He gives his honest opinions to everyone.
Some people like that, others prefer to hear what they want to
hear. Telling people what they want to hear, just because they

want to hear it, is not an option for Ken (ask a few football directors!).

"As for his view of how the game should be played, it would be a fan's idea of Heaven. Talented players, looking to create and play attacking football with no nastiness and no coaches. He'd have everyone playing the type of football that keeps fans talking for days afterwards and 90% would go home with a smile on their faces. I don't think there would be too many clean sheets and definitely no bollockings for trying to do something a little bit out of the ordinary. His ideas might not find too much favour with modern coaches, but he'll never change. That's Ken."

ERIC MULLENDER

Eric Mullender has been involved with Manchester City, in a scouting capacity, for 30 years. He was the man who brought Ryan Giggs, Paul Moulden, Mike Sheron and many others to Maine Road. His earliest memories of Ken Barnes, were of a man in his playing pomp:

"No doubt about it, when Ken played well, Manchester City played well. Simple as that," says Eric.

Eric was a schoolteacher at Haywood School in Bolton when he first got to know Ken:

"I had always loved my football and had played at semi-pro level. I ran teams at the school and really enjoyed it. I took one of the school teams to play in Chorlton and they had a very useful lad on the wing called Peter Barnes.

"The boy could certainly play and then I noticed his dad shouting a bit of encouragement from the sidelines. I saw it was Ken and I must admit that I was a bit awestruck. I'm a dyed-in-the-wool Blue and Ken had been one of my heroes. Still, we got talking and he just mentioned that if I did spot anyone with a bit of talent to let him know. It was very informal at first but later

I started working for him every weekend on a regular basis. He taught me a lot, he had a fantastic instinct for players.

"One of the things I loved about Ken was that once he came to trust you he backed you 100%. I remember bringing Mike Sheron to Maine Road for a trial and he had a nightmare. I was apologising to Ken and saying I didn't know what had happened and Ken just told me not to worry because if I said he could play, then that was good enough for him and he'd get him back in for another look. It was only later that I found out that Mike had played 12 games in 13 days, doing the rounds at club trials. It made such a difference, knowing that someone like Ken had that faith in your judgement.

"We got to be friends over the years. He was a great listener, Ken. We used to talk about all sorts of things, not just football. If he thought you had an area of expertise, he was always keen to ask questions, eager to learn if you like. He's a lovely man, but he is very straight. He hated falsehood and insincerity. He didn't like big mouths or people who shouted the odds. He could spot a phoney at a hundred yards. When I first started going in Ken's room at Maine Road, I listened and learned, but I didn't say much. You never knew who you'd meet in there. One day, Ken took me to one side and said I'd been very quiet. He told me to speak my mind because I had every right to be there. That made me feel ten feet tall, I can tell you. That room was a magical place. When young lads came on match days with their parents, Ken was always so friendly and approachable and his honesty shone through. He never gave them any bull: 'He's got a chance, the boy' usually covered it. There was the added bonus for them of never knowing which football legend was going to walk through the door next.

"As for the kids who did get taken on, well, they had the greatest respect for Ken, or "Mr Barnes" as they called him. Ken and Tony Book had an unbelievable impact on the youngsters. Tony could be very hard on them. He set the standards very high and rightly *so. It's a tough game to get to the top of and Tony was laying the groundwork and setting the standards for these boy's careers. But, I think, Ken just had an instinct for when Tony had pushed them a bit too hard. He would just throw in a few words to the lads, to balance things up, to pick them up if you like.*

"During the week, Ken's office at the ground was like the bootroom at Anfield. Ex-players talking football and putting the world to rights. You had to earn your spurs with Ken to get in there but no wonder former pros and visiting managers and coaches made a beeline for the place.

"I've known Ken Barnes a long time and it's been a privilege. He's taught me a lot about the game and he's taught me a thing or two about life. You won't meet better than Ken. I was proud to be one of his scouts, I really was."

"SKIP" AND THE RETURN OF THE PRODIGAL

Tony Book had joined the coaching staff at Maine Road after a fairy tale time as a player with the club. Brought to City by Malcolm Allison, he found himself on the threshold of a top flight career at an age when most players are thinking about what to do after they hang their boots up. He certainly made up for lost time, captaining the side to four major trophies; the League Championship in 1968, the FA Cup in 1969 and both the League Cup and the European Cup Winners' Cup in 1970.

He might have been untried when he took over as manager from Ron Saunders, but he had a wellspring of goodwill and respect to draw on. He asked Ken to be his assistant, whilst still retaining his scouting role: "Despite his inexperience as a manager, I had an idea that Tony would do a good job. He was a good listener, and was prepared to accept advice. He'd crammed an awful lot into his time at the club and was, of course, one of the cornerstones of all the good things that had happened just a few years before. He knew me well and trusted my judgement of a player. I don't just mean kids but senior pros as well. He put a good side together. In fact, a very good side."

Ken reverted to his scouting role when Tony Book brought in coach Ian McFarlane from Chelsea. Around this time, Chairman Peter Swales decided to implement a system he'd seen at Barcelona; board members to oversee key areas of the club's development. Freddie Pye was given the job of helping Ken Barnes with youth development at Manchester City. Ken was not too impressed with the idea or with his new mentor:

"Some new idea from abroad had got the Chairman's interest, so, in it comes at Maine Road. Typical Swales, really. I got Freddie Pye. Now, Freddie really was larger than life; a character, a true lovable rogue. But, in my opinion, when it came to spotting talent, fuck me, he didn't know his arse from his elbow. He wouldn't know a player if he tripped over one. So, as usual, I just got on with it. I waited for the latest fad to pass and kept looking for players, especially kids, for the club."

One of the kids who came through, was Ken's son Peter:

"I found that a bit difficult at first. I was pleased, of course I was, about his progress. But I tried not to talk about it, in case I got accused of nepotism. I have to say though, the lad could play. He had real pace to go with his trickery and he had excellent control. If I'm honest, I wanted him to go to Leeds with Don (Revie), but Peter was desperate to play for City. He did well and it wasn't easy, because out and out wingers were a dying breed. I was glad too that we played in different positions and in different styles. I didn't want him to have the added pressure of being compared with me. I'm sure there were times when Peter found it as difficult as I did. He had to live with the 'dad at the club' factor. He earned the recognition for what he achieved in his own right, and I was very pleased about that.

The last thing I wanted was to be the monkey on his back. I needn't have worried - he was a fine footballer. In fact, I can remember Bill Shankly shouting to me after a game:

'Ken, that boy of yours looks a player to me.'

'He's got a chance, Bill.'

'A chance? The boy's a real talent, he'll go all the way - mind you, not if he has to run eighty yards every time he gets the ball.'

"Now, Bill knew a thing or two about wingers and he could see the way the wind was blowing, with the emphasis on defensive duties. I was still pleased though, that a football man of his calibre recognised Peter's talent."

Tony Book led Manchester City to League Cup triumph in 1976, with Peter Barnes and Dennis Tueart scoring for the Blues in a 2-1 win over Newcastle United. The following season, the club were runners-up in the league to Liverpool:

"Tony Book put together a side with a nice blend of emerging young players and seasoned pros. He signed Asa (Hartford) on my recommendation. I knew he was a player the minute I saw him. I told Tony to get him signed up and the next thing I know, there are all sorts of stories about his medical condition. I can remember talking to Tony about it:

'What's this bollocks about Asa and his medical?'

'He's got a hole in his heart, Ken.'

'Hole in his arse more like! It 's not done him too much harm so far, has it?'

"Well, they did sign him and he didn't do such a bad job, did he?

"Tony could also still call on great players like Mike Doyle, Alan Oakes and Tommy Booth. Remember too, that some people thought Tony might be a soft touch for the older players, who'd been his team mates. They were wrong because Bookie really did have a bit of steel about him. Francis Lee went to Derby, Mike Summerbee to Burnley. Denis Law packed it in and, of course, he lost the services of Colin Bell to that dreadful knee injury against United. So, Tony dealt with the break up one great team and still managed to put a very useful one together himself.

"Losing Colin was a massive blow. He was a bloody marvellous player. He tried so hard to get back, but he was never going to be the player he had been. Any club in the world would have missed his talent. But even without him, Tony's team won the League Cup and finished second the following year. Things were looking good as far as I could see. Tony was doing a bloody good job from where I was looking, but there were people at the club who thought that the Blues needed a little bit extra; someone to provide that last bit of something, to get the club back to the very top.

"When they told me Malcolm Allison was coming back, as some kind of bloody coaching guru, well, I didn't know what to think. By this time, I was back scouting. Bill Taylor was Tony's first team coach, but he was soon gone when Malcolm came back. I'd had a hand in getting Bill to the club. He'd been at Fulham, as I recall, but was part of the England set-up. When Tony wanted to bring in a coach, it was quite something to get an England coach. I had a word with Don Revie, the England manager, and sounded him out about Taylor. That helped get the wheels in motion.

"Bill was okay - not too coachy, though I did have my doubts when I first met him. I was at Wembley to watch my son, Peter, play for England against the Italians. It was his international debut, and, if I'm honest, I was just a little bit nervous for him. I didn't need to be, he had a great game and was a real handful for them. He'd been up against Gentile, and he wasn't too well known for giving rookies an easy time, was he? Peter had given a real display of the winger's art, against one of the toughest defenders in Europe. I was really proud of how well he'd done. After the game, I got talking to Bill and he asked me, what I thought Peter's best moment in the game had been. Now, I thought Peter had been a real threat to them, going at the full back. But being his dad, you don't go shouting the odds do you? So I just said, that I wasn't really sure. Then Bill came out with a statement that I've never forgotten and still don't see any sense in. He said that Peter's best moment had been chasing back, nicking the ball off an Italian forward and then knocking an easy ball back to the England keeper. I couldn't believe what I was hearing. Peter had just given a real chasing to one of the best, and let's be honest, one of the most cynical defences in the world. A young boy, making his debut, and they hadn't been able to get near him, for the most part. But, according to an international coach, his best moment had been covering back. I don't fuckin' think so! That told me a lot about the way the game was going. Still, Bill did come to City and he did alright. Like I said, though, he was soon out the door when Malcolm got back.

"Malcolm being Malcolm, it was obvious he would want to be in charge of things. With the impact he'd had on Tony's playing career, he was the one person Bookie would find it hard to stand up to. Especially since Swales and his pals thought Malcolm was some kind of magician who could do no wrong. I remember talking to Tony, not long after Malcolm came back:

'He wants to be manager, Ken.'

'What the fuck do you mean? You're the fuckin' manager!'

"Tony just shrugged and said: 'You know what he's like, Ken.'

"It didn't take long for me to see which way the wind was blowing, with Malcolm back at the club. He invited me out for lunch to talk about the players he'd be working with. We talked all day, right through to the early hours. He kept asking me about Gary Owen and he seemed determined to focus on the things Gary wasn't best at, rather than on his qualities - and

Gary had plenty of talent, believe me. I knew that something wasn't right, because he wouldn't let it go. Next morning, Tony collared me and asked how I'd got on with Malcolm. I told him how Malcolm had kept on about Gary. Tony looked a bit sheepish and just said: 'Haven't you heard yet, Ken? Gary's off to the Albion!'

"I thought, fuckin' hell! That's not straight or honest. Malcolm had been playing games with me. It was an amazing time. Malcolm was always larger than life, of course. But now it seemed, that he really had started to believe that he was some kind of miracle worker. I'm sure that he really did believe that he could take a team of unknowns and turn them into world-beaters. I know Alex Ferguson brought through a bunch of kids, who went on to be top Premiership players. But they were all good footballers - we just hadn't heard of them yet. Malcolm shipped out quality and brought in lesser players. That cannot work. Great teams can get by without a great coach - Bob Paisley didn't even have a coach at Liverpool - but no coach can build a great team, unless he has talented players to begin with.

"I couldn't believe it, especially some of the players he brought in. Remember what he said about Barry Silkman and what a player he was going to be? Barry fuckin' Silkman! Steve Daley, Michael Robinson, Steve McKenzie and Bobby Shinton. They either weren't good enough or they were nowhere near worth the money he paid out for them. I think he lost the plot, really. Malcolm was great at instilling confidence and he was a great one for plans and systems but he got so caught up in it all, it got stupid. I still shudder to think how stupid it did get. I can remember following two youngsters down the tunnel after Malcolm's team talk. It was obvious from what they were saying, that they didn't have a bleedin' clue what was expected of them.

"Hindsight's a wonderful thing, of course. Malcolm and Joe

together had been a great team. In combination, they had a chemistry, a magic, that you couldn't pin down, but it was definitely there. Without Joe's moderating influence, Malcolm was a loose cannon. It's sad really. Maybe it just proves the old football saying that you should never go back. That was certainly true of Malcolm and Manchester City.

"I watched what happened and thought it might take the club 10 or 20 years to recover, if it ever did. I retreated into my own job. I would never interfere, but bloody hell, even after all these years I still think back and wonder how it could have happened. The club had seemed to be at the start of something after the League Cup and finishing runners-up in 1977. It was a bloody good team, ready to compete with the best. By the end of 1980, the club was a shambles."

Malcolm Allison and Tony Book left the club, to be replaced by John Bond.

TONY BOOK

Tony Book captained the great Manchester City team of the late 60s/early 70s before going on to manage the side after the sacking of Ron Saunders. His team won the League Cup in 1976 with a 2-1 victory over Newcastle United and he looked set fair for a very successful time as manager at Maine Road when the Blues were runners - up to Liverpool in the League in the 76/77 season. The return of Malcolm Allison and the ensuing debacle, cost Tony his job.

He later returned to the club under John Bond to work with Ken Barnes: *"I don't remember Ken as a player, if I'm being honest. It wasn't like today, when you can watch anyone on the box. The opportunities to see the top players back in the 50s, especially down in the south west where I lived, were very limited.*

"*I first got to know him, when Joe Mercer brought him to Maine Road. I could tell right off, that he was a real football man. It was obvious he had a lot of experience and he was certainly very expansive when it came to talking about the game. I saw him, I suppose, as a bit of an anti-establishment figure. If you look at any period of time in the history of football you always find that certain ideas hold sway at a given time. Certain systems and tactics seem to be the current fashion. It's always been that way. It made no difference to Ken. He believed what he believed and if that went against the grain of the current football wisdom, it made no difference. If someone was being touted as the best thing since sliced bread a lot of people would go along with the flow rather than stick their head above the parapet. Ken wasn't capable of that. His honesty and the strength of his beliefs, meant he had to say what he thought. He couldn't just nod and keep his real thoughts to himself, that wasn't Ken at all.*

"*I loved his honesty. Once you knew him, you could trust him without a moment's hesitation. It sounds a bit dramatic maybe, but I really did feel I could trust him with my life.*

"*When I got the manager's job at Manchester City, Ken was one of my bedrocks. It wasn't just that I trusted him, totally, as a man, but also his knowledge was absolutely invaluable to me and the club. He was a brilliant scout. He didn't get it wrong very often, whether it was kids or senior pros he was watching. We were both football men. We loved the game and being involved with it, but neither of us had any time for the politics that surround the football.*

"*When I came back to the club, to work with Ken and the club's youngsters, I can only describe it as a magical time. I like to think we had a chemistry. I was very hard, very demanding. I set the standards very high and really pushed the lads to achieve their potential. Occasionally, Ken would step in with a word or two. He had this amazing knack of knowing just when it was time to lighten the mood or ease the pressure. In some ways, we were like two bits of a jigsaw; different, but somehow they fit together. Ken had a real gift for spotting potential in youngsters and he had a magical ability to make them, and their parents, feel that Maine Road was a truly special place. Maybe he wasn't so good at the details. I was the one who tended to get the forms signed and the niceties sorted out. It worked though. If you look at the talent that emerged during that period, I really feel that everyone involved in the youth set up, not just Ken and me, should be really proud of what was achieved.*

"I said it was a magical time and it really was. The hub of it all was Ken's office at Maine Road. When I think of the good times we shared in there, I really do feel it was a special period for a lot of people. The first thing that comes to mind is laughter. It was a happy place to be. Ken was brilliant with all the staff in the kitchen and with those who worked in admin. It was a fun place to work but the results showed that it was a very effective operation. You can afford to enjoy your work, when the results are there for all to see.

"I know for a fact that Peter Swales sometimes wondered what was going on in Ken's office. He thought it was some kind of drinking den for ex-pros. In terms of value for money it was, probably, the most productive room in the ground.

"Ken is a real football man to the core and he knows how to enjoy life. That's why football people love him."

PETER BARNES

It is never easy for the footballing son of a footballing father. Father-son comparisons may be unfair, but they are also inevitable; especially when both have played for the same club. As a consequence, there can be no greater testament to the footballing talent of Peter Barnes, than the simple fact that he is not remembered for comparison with Ken, but for his own outstanding exploits at club and international level. According to Peter, Ken was very encouraging of all his sons in their early football endeavours. But there were limits:

"We were all football daft. My two brothers, Keith and Michael, loved the game just as I did. We used to play all the time in the street, in the park or in the garden. Playing in the garden was the problem. My dad loved his garden and if we were playing in the back, mum would always tell us to be careful of his roses. Well, we always started with the best of intentions, but like all kids we'd get caught up in the game and there would be casualties. I remember dad coming home one day and finding his roses in a right state. He was fuming. He grabbed the ball and put a knife through it! Another time, he kicked the ball out of the garden and over the wall into the schoolyard. He always calmed down and bought us another one the next day. In fairness to dad, if his roses weren't at stake, he was always encouraging all three of us as players.

"I can just remember him as a player. It was after he left City, of course, but he certainly used to talk a lot. He would never stop talking out on the pitch. It was as if he could see the whole game in his head, and he was explaining and telling people what to do, to make things unfold as he thought they should. Of course, it was a long time ago, he might have just been moaning!

"When I signed for City, I think my dad would have preferred me to go to Leeds with Don Revie. Looking back, I can understand why. With me being the son of a former City player, it was never going to be easy. If you do well, you're getting picked because of who your dad is, that sort of thing. But I had my mind set on Maine Road. I'm sure there were people who thought it, even if they didn't say it, that I was only there because my dad was Ken Barnes. I like to think I did enough to justify myself in my time there. Being honest though, it probably did make life easier that I was a totally different player to my dad. I don't believe I got any special treatment because he was there; he would have gone up the wall if I had. He took an interest in my career, of course he did,

but what father doesn't?

"He always tried to keep my feet on the ground. He wasn't critical, he just wanted to make sure that I kept a realistic view, when things happened so fast for me at such a young age. I remember him and my mum coming to Wembley to watch my England debut against Italy. I did pretty well. I was up against Claudio Gentile and I didn't do too badly. I got past him a few times. I remember after the game, one of the coaches, Bill Taylor, told my dad my best moment had been when I tackled back. I thought dad was going to hit him!

"When dad was chief scout at City he had a great set up. He built up a really good team of scouts, who all seemed to think the world of him and his office at the ground was the stuff of legend. You never knew who you'd meet in there. Talk about open all hours - and there was always a cup of tea to be had. I can recall Bernard Halford telling dad to keep an eye on the milk bill. Can you believe it? This was the club that'd paid a million and a half for Steve Daley and dad gets pulled up for using too much milk. Incredible.

"When Peter Reid decided dad was surplus to requirements, it hit him really hard. The club and the game were his life. He was delighted to be asked to go back. The second time they decide to get rid of him, well, I'm sure it still hurt his pride, but not as much. After 50 years, I think he felt he'd done his bit. I knew the game would call him back eventually though. That's why I'm delighted that he's got involved with my half sister, Karen, in developing grass roots and school football out in Malaysia. I've been out there and I can see how quickly he gets immersed in it all. It's the perfect chance to test his coaching beliefs. It might not quite be a blank sheet, but it's a lot better opportunity than he'd ever get over here.

"He thought his football days were over and now he's a star out there and rubbing shoulders with royalty. It doesn't surprise me, if I'm honest. The game will never lose its fascination for my dad."

SANITY RESTORED

John Bond arrived from Norwich City in October 1980 and immediately set about introducing some older heads into a struggling side. He brought in full back Bobby McDonald and the vastly experienced winger Tommy Hutchison from Coventry City and also added tough tackling midfielder Gerry Gow from Bristol City. The improvement was immediate. After taking just 4 points from their first 12 games, the Blues lost only 3 of the next 16. Along with a respectable 12th place in the league, the club reached the semi-final of the League Cup, losing out to Liverpool. John Bond also got to lead his side out at Wembley for the Centenary FA Cup Final. City should have won the Saturday game, which ended 1-1 and then lost a remarkable replay 3-2, a match decided by one of the most talked about FA Cup goals ever, scored by Ricky Villa.

Despite the Wembley disappointment, it had been an exciting season for Bond and his side. Having brought a bit of stability to Maine Road, Bond's next objective was to build a club and a side capable of matching the best. The signing of Martin O'Neill and the £1million plus acquisition of Trevor Francis augured well for the future, as did the return to Maine Road of Tony Book, to work with Ken Barnes on the scouting set-up. Asa Hartford also came back after spells with Nottingham Forest and Everton.

Sadly, the club was finding it increasingly difficult to back the manager's ambitions on the playing side and, at the same time, find the money to redevelop the stadium.

Trevor Francis went to Italy after just one season with the Blues and after a mediocre season in 1981/82 and an indifferent start to the following campaign John Bond resigned, amid stories of an uneasy relationship with certain board members. Sadly, all the expectation generated by his early impact evaporated.

Ken Barnes was sorry to see him go, "I liked him and his ideas about football. He believed that football was, essentially, a simple game and he certainly wasn't hung up on systems. He took some obvious but very effective steps to sort out the mess that Malcolm had left. And things were looking very positive with some of his signings. Trevor Francis was a very talented lad, though sadly for City and the fans, who loved the glimpses they did see of his quality, he didn't play much. And bringing Asa back was an excellent move. He also brought back Tony (Book), which was fair enough because Tony had gone when Malcolm went and I felt he'd paid the price for what Malcolm had done; caught in the crossfire if you like. Let's face it, Tony's own record, before Malcolm came back, was excellent.

"John could be blunt and I thought, sometimes, he could be a bit too hard on young kids, to the point of denting their confidence. I remember once, I walked past as he was giving one of the kids a right blasting, I mean a real bollocking. I felt I had to say something, even if there might be a price to pay. I collared him later and told him straight:

'What the fuck are you doing talking to the kid like that? You could destroy him, for fuck's sake! What would you have said if someone had spoken to your lad like that when he was just starting out in the game?'

"John just walked away. The next morning I was half expecting to get the call to clear my desk, thinking I might have been out of order. After all, he was the manager and I was only the scout. Next thing, John walked into my office, threw his hands up and apologised. He said I'd been right and he'd been wrong and believe me, in an ego business like football, there aren't many who would do that. Bugger me, next thing I know he's sorted out a pay rise for me. The money was nice, of course it was, but the fact that he was prepared to hold his hands up told me all I needed to know about John Bond. We'll never know now, but I really think he could have gone on to achieve a lot at the club, if the circumstances had been different.

"I was shocked when he left, I have to say. Of course, I heard the stories about his relationship with some of the board. Things like that happen in football and in life. After all, football people are still people. But I really think things could have been very different under John."

JOHN BOND

John Bond took over as manager at Manchester City following the disastrous second spell at the club of Malcolm Allison. Arriving from Norwich City, it was not an easy situation that he found himself in, *"The club was in trouble on the pitch and I don't think I would be surprising too many people if I say I wasn't the first choice of some of the directors. I knew how to tackle the stuff on the park and started to get to grips with that. I was still working out the politics when I met Ken Barnes. Of course, I'd seen him play. He was as slow as a carthorse, but what a brain for the game. I remember me and Ken played together in a testimonial at Southport. Ken was right-half and I played on the right wing. Now, I always thought of myself as a decent passer of a football, but after an hour he still hadn't passed to me. Not once. Maybe he didn't think I was as good as I thought I was!*

"When I got to City, he was the chief scout and he'd been back at Maine Road for ten years. You never know quite what to expect when you're the new boy in that situation and someone's been there that long. You never know if they'll resent you and any changes you try to make. With Ken, if I'm being honest, I could not believe what I was seeing. His honesty took your breath away, especially some of the things he said to the Chairman and the directors. I soon realised that Ken was just being himself. With

him, it was the players first and foremost and woe betide any director who forgot that. A summons from on high didn't carry a lot of weight with Ken.

"As I got to know him, I really took to Ken, because he was so totally honest. If Ken believed in you he gave you his best and his backing 100%, no question about it. In the circumstances I found myself it was great to have someone I could trust absolutely. Don't misunderstand me, Ken was as honest with me as he was with Peter Swales and that meant I got it straight between the eyes as much as the Chairman did. We had our arguments but you knew with Ken there was never a hidden agenda. He didn't function like that. He gave me a right bollocking once and when I thought about it, I realised that what he was mad about was right. I sorted him out with the only pay rise he got in all his time as chief scout. I think that surprised him a bit - he thought I was going to sack him! That was the great bonus of dealing with Ken. You might have a blazing row but once the dust settled, you had to give it some thought. Because, deep down, you knew he wouldn't have said it unless he meant it.

"We have a lot of our football views in common. We both believe that football is a simple game - if you get the right players. He was a great judge of a player. You don't need me to tell you that, just look at his track record. They tell me he's mellowed with age. That's as maybe. All I know is that if I want to get Ken going, I just have to phone him up and suggest that David Beckham is better than Tom Finney. See how mellow he is at that suggestion!

"Ken was one of the best things about my time at Manchester City. Like I say, I couldn't believe what he was like when I first got to Maine Road, but I soon learned what a smashing bloke he was. He still is. Ken's brilliant - I love him to bits."

HOLDING THE FORT

Following the sudden departure of John Bond, assistant manager John Benson was appointed as caretaker manager. He could not stop the club's tumble down the league and City were relegated on the last day of the season, losing 1-0 at home to Luton Town. Raddy Antic scored the only goal of the game for a Luton side captained by future City manager Brian Horton. Nearly 43,000 turned out to see the club that had been within minutes of winning the Centenary FA Cup Final just 2 years before, drop out of the top flight.

Ken Barnes had good reason to be grateful to Benson and rates him a good football man:

"I liked John. He knew his football and he was honest and straight. Let's face it, here we are 20 odd years later and he's still in the game and that must tell you something. I'm not sure if he was cut out to be a manager though. No shame in that of course. I know, from personal experience, that it doesn't suit everyone. In any case, Peter Swales seemed to be obsessed with the idea of a 'big name'. So, even if John had taken them into Europe, he could still have been out on his ear!

"One time though, I had good reason to be grateful to John and his instincts. I found myself in dispute with someone brought to the club by a previous manager. He said some things about me that were absolute rubbish and it wasn't in my nature to just let him get away with what was, basically, a character assassination. It ended up with the pair of us in John Benson's office. It was a real stand off, with John Benson slap bang in the middle. I was fuming and told John:

'Look John, he obviously wants my job, so fuck it, he can have it!'

"John looked at me and said, 'Stay where you are Ken, you're going nowhere, he is.'"

Ken recalls the incident clearly and knows that if Benson had not backed him, his time at City would have been drastically curtailed:

"No doubt about it, I would have gone and my time at Maine Road would have finished there and then. John Benson believed me and put his trust in me. If he hadn't, I'd have gone, no doubt about it whatsoever."

It's a moot point as to whether John Benson would have been offered the manager's job, on a permanent basis, if the Blues had survived. They didn't and he was sacked.

In his quest for a big name to lead City back to glory, Chairman Peter Swales looked north of the border to Glasgow and Celtic legend Billy McNeill.

BILLY AND THE KIDS

Billy McNeill had assumed almost mythical status to Glasgow Celtic fans, having captained the side to European Cup triumph in 1967 before going on to manage the club. He was, undoubtedly, the kind of big name appointment Peter Swales was seeking, but was also an unknown quantity in terms of English club management.

McNeill found it hard to settle at first, missing Glasgow and finding it difficult to get his bearings in a comparatively alien football environment. He was also surprised at just how bad things were, financially, at Maine Road. Based on the club's recent spending exploits McNeill had expected some money would be available to buy players. Not so. Whatever his personal difficulties, Billy McNeill was astute enough to seek the counsel of a man who knew more than most about the club:

"I liked Billy very much. A first class man. He found it difficult to settle at first. He was a bit homesick, I think, and it was his first job in England. I got the impression when he came to see me that he felt he'd been misled about the financial position at City. From Scotland, it must have seemed like a club with money to burn, but that wasn't the case now. Billy asked me about the Chairman and I told him I had nothing to do with him and wanted to keep it that way because the Chairman was a ****. I really think that Billy was bemused at how bad the money situation was:

'Ken, they're telling me there's nothing at all in the pot.'

'You've picked the wrong day to come to me for sympathy, Bill - I've had my fuckin' phone cut off this morning!'

"In fairness to Billy, he got stuck in and started to find his feet. It can't have been easy because he was missing Glasgow and living out of a suitcase in Manchester. I think he came close to packing it in in the early days. He brought in Jimmy Frizzell as his assistant. Frizz knew all about running a club with no money, from his time with Oldham Athletic. They brought in a few bargain basement players - they had to, they didn't have any money for anything else: Derek Parlane, Neil McNab, Jim Tolmie. There were a few rumblings, as I recall, about signings Jocks, but what else could they do? If you haven't got the money for the players you want, you have to trawl through the players you know. Most importantly of all perhaps, you have to trawl through the players you know you can get and then hope they will do a job."

City missed out on promotion in McNeill's first season by one place (and 10 points). They were promoted the following year and in the 1985/86 season they not only survived in the First Division, but also made the final of the Full Members Cup. They lost 5-4 to Chelsea at Wembley.

If the first team was making progress under Billy McNeill, the City youngsters were causing a fair bit of excitement too. In April 1986 the youth team beat Manchester United 3-1 in the FA Youth Cup Final. The City side included Paul Lake, Steve

Redmond, Ian Brightwell, Andy Hinchcliffe, David White, Paul Moulden and Ian Scott, all of whom went on to play for City's first team. A fantastic tribute to Ken Barnes' ability to spot talent, you might think. Ken himself is more modest about his scouting ability:

"We were a bit lucky, really, to get so many of the boys through to the senior side. Circumstances played a part of course. With no money, the club had to throw the kids in. It might have been different if they'd been in a position to buy established players. They were a great set of lads, who'd grown up together. Of course I was proud of them, but I still say there was some luck involved. You don't see it very often, where so many go on to play at the highest level.

"I suppose I'd have to say that Paul Lake was the jewel in the crown. When I first saw him as a young laddie of about 13, I knew straight away he was a real talent. He was going flat out and had a ball dropping over his shoulder and he set himself and volleyed it into the back of the net. I remember thinking to myself, right then, that I'd seen enough, he was a player. As he grew up, he reminded me of Colin Bell and I can pay him no greater tribute than that. He could do everything. He could pass and tackle, he was good in the air. He could graft, but most of all he was a smart player. He had vision, he could see things that other players couldn't. Paul could have played anywhere. It was an absolute tragedy that we never got to see the best of him. I'm sure he would have gone on to be one of the true City greats, I really do believe that.

"Steve Redmond was a good player. But what a lot of people might not know is that, as a youngster, he was great goalscorer, a real natural. He was so strong and he had 2 great feet. I felt he had a real future as a front player. Then, bugger me, the next thing is they're turning him into a centre back. I've never understood it - goalscorers are always at a premium. Centre halves, by comparison, are ten a penny. We find a laddie with the talent to play up there and then shove him in at the back. Bloody unbelievable really.

"Paul Moulden was a goal scoring machine, with great control and touch and a good football brain. The only thing lacking was a yard of pace. Paul had the talent to achieve a lot more than he did in the game and people always say it was down to that lack of pace. Maybe so, but sometimes you need a bit of luck as well and I still feel that, with a bit of good fortune, things could have been very different for him.

"David White had a good career in the game, of course. As a kid he was strong and direct, very quick. He wasn't a tricky winger like we'd seen in the past. He blasted past people with pace rather than licking them with a bit of pure skill. He was a good crosser of the ball. Maybe David lacked a little bit of football savvy sometimes but he knew his strengths, he played to them and they served him well.

"Ian Brightwell was a lovely lad with a fantastic attitude. I don't think he was capable of giving less than his best - it just wasn't in his nature. Good defender, strong in the tackle and had a bit of pace about him. He didn't have as much to offer in an attacking sense, but from a manager's perspective, a real asset. His attitude was exceptional and you couldn't hope to meet a nicer man.

"Andy Hinchcliffe was very fast and a good passer of a ball, especially for a defender. He had a great left foot and that has always been at a premium - as much so then as it is now. For some reason, Howard Kendall didn't rate him and he moved on. But, I still believe to this day, that he could have been first choice left back here for ten years or more. He's not done too badly for himself in the game has he?

"Ian Scott was one, I thought, might have done more in the game. He was a decent player with a bit of vision. He saw things early, which I always liked. Yes, I thought he would be a good player. It didn't quite work out for him and I was sorry about that, because he certainly had the talent."

It was an understandable source of pride for Ken to see his signings reach the first team, but his efforts were not always as highly valued as might be expected. Justifiable pride came with a great sense of frustration that a club, with so few resources to go out and sign big name players any longer, still failed to appreciate the efforts being made to provide an alternative source of talent.

In the mid 80s, his frustration led to a memo to the board about a lack of understanding of what he was trying to do. Ken was a great believer in making Manchester City a special place for young potential players and their parents. He liked to invite the lads and their families to Maine Road on match days, to savour the atmosphere and get a feel for the place and the people who made it tick. Most people would see the wisdom of that approach. But Ken was asked by the board if it was wise to use up 20 odd tickets at every home game and then push the boat out by offering his guests a bite of lunch.

Ken's memo - couched in, by Ken's standards, remarkably diplomatic terms - argued the case for using the tickets on youngsters who might well represent the future of the club as opposed to giving them to friends of the board, who would never kick a ball in anger:

"I honestly couldn't fuckin' believe it! The proof of what we were trying to do was out there on the park. To me, it was just common sense. In a very competitive market - all the top clubs were after the best kids - I wanted us to be the best. I wanted to make Maine Road a special place for the young lads and their parents. It wasn't fuckin' rocket science. I can still remember a certain look you would see on a dad's face. You just knew he couldn't wait for Monday, to get to work and tell his mates he'd met Colin Bell. If a lad did the rounds of 4 or 5 clubs, I wanted his best memories to be of Manchester City. Bugger me, I'm being asked to justify a few tickets and sandwiches. What the fuck else were they going to do with them? Give them to their croneys? I used to despair sometimes. Some of them used to swan about and they didn't know their arse from their elbow when it came to football. They were all supposed to be so canny and astute, but they couldn't see the sense of what I was doing. It was because of things like that, I had as little as possible to do with them. In truth, I was never going to get on with Peter Swales. He loved wheeling and dealing and he was the type who thought he had the right to an opinion on anything happening at the club, even if he didn't have a clue about the real situation. Apart from the ticket thing he collared me once about the amount of drink being used in my office. As you might expect, this led to a lively exchange of views:

'I'm a bit concerned about the drinks bill for your office, Ken. What are you doing in there, running a nightclub?'

'Running a fuckin' nightclub? For your information, I'm working. Entertaining people, who might help the future of this football club. The parents of lads who could be players here one day. Not that you'd know, because you never show your fuckin' face in my office to talk to those people and you're supposed to be the Chairman of this place. If you want to question my drinks bill, let's have a look at yours for your mates. How many of them are likely to be playing in the first team in a couple of years?'"

The increasingly competitive market, to secure the services of the best young players, meant that financial inducements were, increasingly, part of the equation. Ken was not happy about the situation, but knew that it was a reality to be faced, "I never mentioned money in my dealings with parents, until it became obvious that money was on the table from another club. What could you do? You couldn't ignore it. Nobody was admitting anything, but as clubs looked to get the best kids, some of the parents were plenty sharp enough to know the score. I'd been working to sign a young lad who did end up at

Maine Road. I called at his house and his dad was looking at me a bit funny. I'd got to know him pretty well and I knew something was going on. I asked him if he had something to tell me. He said that another club had offered them ten thousand pounds, if their son signed, and that another club had offered to top that. I asked him what he expected me to do. He said he just wanted to have a bit of money in the bank, 'For the lad's sake, Ken, not for me.' He did make it clear that his son wanted to play for City. I reported back to Peter Swales and remember, he'd never seen the kid play, but he had to have his twopennorth:

'Who does he think he is Ken? The next Duncan Edwards?'

'I'm not saying that. But I am telling you, that if you want a lad who will definitely make the first team at Maine Road, then that is what you are up against.'

"That was Peter Swales. It didn't matter if it was an area he knew nothing about, he still felt he had to have his say. It was like a compulsion. I suppose it is for people like that.

"There was another fly in that particular ointment jar. I got a call from the headmaster at the laddie's school. He told me that the boy's sportsmaster thought he should be playing with his schoolmates in his last year there, rather than for City. I told the headmaster that, in football terms, the boy would be going backwards playing for the school, rather than for City's 'A' team or reserves. He still wasn't convinced, so I painted him a stark picture. I asked him outright if he could guarantee the lad a job at the end of the school year because if he couldn't, I could."

The player did sign for Manchester City and did play regular first team football, before moving to another top club.

Ken was also on the lookout for potential first team players for Billy McNeill, and, in that role, he watched a game involving Blackpool. He was watching a particular player, but also running the rule over Blackpool, who City had drawn in the

FA Cup:

"It was, without doubt, one of the worst games of football I had seen - anywhere, ever. Putrid. Afterwards, I couldn't recall a single passage of play that would have justified the title 'professional football'. Nevertheless, I did fill in a match report for Billy and I put in it that I would show my arse in Piccadilly if we didn't beat Blackpool in the Cup. Billy read the report and told me to change it so that it said the players would show their arses in Piccadilly if we didn't beat Blackpool in the Cup. I remember Billy pinning the report up in the dressing room. The players had a good laugh about it. Of course, City being City, we lost to them and, no, the players didn't show their arses - they should have though, losing to that lot."

Billy McNeill was growing increasingly frustrated by the tight purse strings at Maine Road. Pleas for patience were hard for the Scot and when Freddie Pye was appointed 'Director In Charge Of Team Affairs', the writing was, well and truly, on the wall. McNeill and the larger than life Pye did not get on and seemed disinclined to try. Early in the 1986/87 campaign McNeill left, for one disastrous season with Aston Villa, before heading back north of the border. Ken Barnes was sad to see him go:

"When Bill told me he was off to the Villa, I asked him what the bloody hell he wanted to go there for. But he'd just had enough of trying to do things on the cheap and felt he'd gone as far as he could at Maine Road, unless he got some money. I was at Villa Park once and Doug Ellis told me he thought Billy had used Villa. I was bloody fuming. I put him right. Billy McNeill was as straight as they come. I had a lot of time for Bill. I think he did a great job, in difficult circumstances, and if he'd had a fraction of the money that some had been allowed to spend here, he could have done great things. I still keep in touch with him; a real football man and a top class fellah"

Jimmy Frizzell moved into the Manager's chair.

BILLY MCNEILL

When Billy McNeill took over as manager of Manchester City, it was his first job in England. As he found his feet at Maine Road, he found a friend and ally in Ken Barnes:

"Ken was invaluable. I knew he'd been a great player, but meeting him for the first time, I knew he was my type of man. Ken is what I would call a man's man, though he can certainly charm the ladies. We hit it off right from our first meeting. I'll make no bones about it, I found it difficult to settle at first. It was my first job down in England and it took me a while to get used to life in Manchester. The other thing I had to come to terms with was the financial situation at Maine Road when I got there. Let's just say that it was a lot worse than I had been led to believe, a lot worse. So, there I was, the new kid, taking on a massive new job in a strange city. There were times when I felt like heading back home and in that situation, someone like Ken was an absolute Godsend. Just to have someone you knew you could trust absolutely. In any football club, there's any amount of politics and wheeler dealing going on. Ken was never part of that, he was incapable of it. It wasn't in his make up. Whenever I was wondering what I'd got myself into, Ken just made me laugh. He was great company and breathtakingly honest, whoever he was talking to. I found that refreshing, though I'm not sure if all the directors would say the same. Anyone that straight was alright in my book. No backstabbing or badmouthing, it was all up front with Ken. If he thought it, he said it. You might not like it, but you knew he meant it.

"His football knowledge was amazing and how he managed to get all those great kids to sign for City I'll never know. Make no mistake about it, all the top clubs were after them. That City did so well, in so competitive a market, was down to Ken. It wasn't just me though, Manchester City had a lot to thank Ken for. The

financial position was so bad, I really believe that without all that talent he found, the club could have gone under. He did as much as anyone to save Manchester City.

"*Life was never dull with Ken around. I remember when they opened a new restaurant at Maine Road and decided to use his office to store all the sweets on match day. Not a good idea. Ken brought a youngster and his parents to have a look round on the Saturday and when he walked into his office, with them in tow, the place was groaning under the weight of the puddings. Ken, not best pleased, went storming off to see Peter Swales, 'Hey you, what the fuck is that all about? I'm trying to sign this lad for your fuckin' club, trying to show him and his parents what a special place this is and I'm up to my fuckin' arse in blancmange and whipped cream!'*

"*I learned very quickly, that Ken was absolutely on top of the scouting job. There cannot be anybody in the game with a better address book than him. He had a way of making his point, so that you were in no doubt where he stood. We were talking once and I just happened to suggest, that there had to be some talent in the lower divisions, if you just looked hard enough. Ken looked at me and said he'd take me to a game that night. It was the old Fourth Division, Prenton Park, Tranmere Rovers against York City. It was a cold night with a very blustery wind blowing across the pitch. It wasn't easy to play but for the whole of the first half, the ball hardly touched the floor. Bang, bang, bang, back and forth, absolutely awful. Ken never said a word. At half time, he turned to me and just said, 'Seen enough?' As we were walking back to the car, he looked at me, shrugged and said, 'Even God couldn't pick a player out of that lot.' It made me laugh all the way back to the car, but I never questioned his judgement again after that.*

"*I mentioned Ken's honesty. I don't think he would ever change, in fact, I don't think he could ever change, even if it was the Queen he was talking to. He's true to himself. Ken swears a lot, but he swears whoever he's with. He has no airs and graces, he's always the same. A couple of years ago, I invited him up to Scotland for a charity function. It was quite an up market event and there were plenty of people there with a few shillings. Ken was in amongst them, effing and jeffing as only he can. I remember thinking to myself, I wonder what they'll make of him. Needless to say, he had them eating out of his hand. They're always asking me when he's coming back up. Like everyone else, they recognised just what a genuine bloke he is. Alright, you get a few expletives along the way, but that's just Ken.*

"Ken is one of my favourite people in the game because he's so genuine. I'm not saying anything you don't already know, if I say the game has more than its share of rogues and conmen. In comparison, Ken Barnes is a breath of fresh air. He might take no prisoners and he certainly does give it you right between the eyes. But if he says something, stop and listen, because you know he means it and you will almost certainly learn something.

"No doubt about it, Ken Barnes is one of the greats; great player, great scout, great bloke."

JAMIE HOYLAND

Jamie Hoyland began his playing career with Manchester City and was signed for the club by Ken Barnes. He remembers Ken with a combination of respect and affection:

"He was fantastic with the kids. I had the chance to go to a few clubs but the set up at Maine Road was different. It really was a special place and a lot of that special atmosphere, I felt, was down to Ken and his staff. I was talking to Simmo (Paul Simpson) about it. When were training with the club as kids, we used to stay at a hotel on Wilmslow Road and we just couldn't wait to get going in the morning. You just wanted to be part of what was going on at City because it really did have a kind of magic about it. Ken had an unbelievable charisma. You just felt so relaxed in

his company. Running up the stairs to his office, you always had a sense of excitement. Ken would be there, with a fag on the go and he certainly used to swear a bit. Somehow, that seemed quite exciting when you were 14. But he could make you believe in yourself. I was always concerned about my lack of pace, but Ken was always telling me: 'Don't worry about pace. You can play, you can control it and pass it, so don't worry about pace.'

"My dad had told me all about Ken, because he'd played against him in the 50s. I knew he'd been a great player, so I was a bit in awe of him at first. He really took an interest in all the kids, even after we left Maine Road. Whenever you saw him, it was obvious that he'd been keeping up to date with what you were doing. I think that, to Ken, we would always be his boys, no matter who we were actually playing for.

"I always knew I could trust him. If Ken said you were a good player, he meant it - he wouldn't be saying the opposite, to someone else, when you walked out the door. I looked up to him and wanted to be like him, I still do. Don't get me wrong. He was no saint but he was dead honest. He said what he thought but he meant what he said. He wasn't one for shouting and bawling at the kids but he had a way of letting you know if he wasn't happy with you. I'm not sure why but it seemed to carry a lot more weight than any full blown rollocking.

"When you look back, you realise just how good Ken was at all aspects of his job. You tell me someone who could spot a player better than he could. All those players he signed who went on to have good careers in the game. There was no luck involved. He didn't pick hundreds in the hope a few might make it. He had an unbelievable knowledge of the game and nobody could spot a player better than Ken. Nowadays, with his eye for talent, he'd probably be an agent worth millions.

"Even now, I use a lot of the things we learned at City as a yardstick in the game. Not just stuff we learned from Ken, of course, but also from people like Tony Book. Ken and Bookie *taught us, and instilled in us, the basics principles that are the cornerstones of building anything worthwhile in the game. It's only as you get a bit older and wiser, you see just how important men like them have been in your life.*

"Ken Barnes is one of those people who puts a smile on your face, whenever you see him. He's made a fantastic contribution to Manchester City, as a player and as a scout. But perhaps most importantly of all, he's just a smashing bloke."

PAUL LAKE

Ken Barnes spotted Paul Lake as a youngster playing for Denton Boys and he was immediately impressed by an exceptional talent. After playing for City's nursery team and being part of the FA Youth Cup winning side of 1986, Paul made rapid strides into the first team at Maine Road. Sadly, his playing career was curtailed by a serious knee injury and after a long battle for fitness he eventually had to concede defeat. City fans were left to wonder what might have been for a player who, Ken believed, was destined to be the Colin Bell of his generation. Paul, to his great credit, has dealt with the disappointment and gone on to make a second career as a physiotherapist. At the time of writing he is working at Macclesfield Town. He believes that Ken Barnes had a great impact on him as a footballer and as a person:

"Ken Barnes, Tony Book and, to a lesser extent, Glyn Pardoe were the greatest influences in my football career. Bookie and Ken seemed to have the good cop/bad cop routine off to perfection. Tony was quite strict and set very high standards and for the most part that was fine, but if Ken thought he was being too hard on a youngster, he'd have a blazing row with Tony:

'Hey, did you never make a mistake then? What the fuck do you know anyway? You were only a full back.'

"Tony was more one for detail and more analytical maybe, but Ken just had a way of making you feel ten feet tall. Tony rarely missed a game but I can remember he did miss one once and Ken gave us the team talk. He walked in with his usual fag on the go and said:

'Go out and play. Express yourselves, you're better than them, so get out there and fuckin' enjoy it.'

"That was it. We came in at half time winning 3-0 and he just walked in and said, 'Do the same again. I told you you were better than this lot. Enjoy yourselves.' Team talk over.

"We won about 5 or 6 nil. We were only kids, but we could have given Real Madrid a game that day, or at least Ken had us believing we could.

"Ken didn't have a lot of time for directors. It was always football and, more particularly, footballers first and foremost. If he was talking to a young kid and someone like Peter Swales called him over, he always told him he'd have to wait because he was talking to someone who might be important to the club's future. You can imagine how that went down with board members. Ken didn't have any time for them and he never tried to hide it. It was very different with his kids. He treated us like sons really. You always felt you were important to him. We all had immense respect for him. I think I was in the first team before I stopped calling him Mr Barnes. He told me to call him Ken. I can't explain how good that made me feel. It was like I had been accepted as a player. All the youngsters called him that but it was out of genuine respect, we didn't resent it. I bet when Steve Lomas comes back to City, he'll call Ken "Mr Barnes", until Ken tells him otherwise.

"As for Ken's office at Maine Road, it was quite a thing to get invited in there. Once the smoke cleared, it always seemed to be full of ex-players and to get in to join them was brilliant. It was another indication that you were a proper footballer.

"It's funny but I've always believed that the eyes are the mirror of the soul and when Ken got talking about football, his eyes used

to really blaze with passion and love for the game and we'd get caught up in it. If I bumped into him at Platt Lane and we got talking, I'd get carried along and I'd look at my watch and 2 hours would have flown by. Ken could hold you spellbound when he talked about the game.

"I love Ken, he's a really brilliant man with an unbelievable knowledge of the game. His influence on the kids at City was immense, beyond measure."

IAN BRIGHTWELL

Ian Brightwell, known as "Bob" to one and all, was one of eight members of the 1986 FA Youth Cup winning side who went on to play for the first team at Manchester City. After a long and distinguished career of over 300 games with the Blues, Ian moved on to Coventry City in 1998. Ian is part of a highly successful sporting family, with both his parents being Olympic medallists and his brother, David, a fellow professional footballer. Despite his own footballing achievements and an association going back 20 years, Ian still regards Ken Barnes with something approaching awe:

"No doubt about it. If I get the chance to go to City and I bump into Ken, I automatically call him Mr Barnes. He was always that when we were kids and I still feel it is thing to do now, even though I'm in my 30s. We have a little laugh about it now, of course, but I'd never take liberties.

"When I first started to go down to City in the school holidays, Ken was always there, always making sure that things were right for us. I took to him straight away and I know that my mum and dad did too. You knew, right from the off, that this was a man you could trust and, obviously, that was important to any parent, not just mine. Having been athletes at the very highest level themselves, I think they knew how critical the early influences are

on someone looking to make a go of sport at a serious level.

"Ken's a truly nice fella, always ready with a joke and a word of encouragement. You really felt he wanted you to do well and that made you want to do well for him. His first question after a game was always 'Did you enjoy it?' He wanted us to be happy. He always encouraged you to do what you were good at and to play to your strengths. Obviously, in the professional game, you expect to have your faults picked out and worked on but, sometimes, you just needed someone to remind you that you were there because you could actually play a bit. He had a real instinct for knowing when you needed a bit of a lift.

"Along with my parents, the people we worked under back in my early days at Maine Road - Ken, Tony Book and Glyn Pardoe - had a massive influence on my life. It would be fair to say that they put me where I am today. I owe them a lot.

"They really were legends. The part they played in finding and developing young talent was unbelievable really. When you look back at the kids Ken found for the club and the careers they went on to have at City or elsewhere, I really don't feel that people appreciate just how significant his contribution to the club was.

"Ken, Mr Barnes, is a smashing bloke and a real football man. I can't speak highly enough of what he did for me."

FRIZZ

Jimmy Frizzell took over in September 1986, just 7 games into the new season. He had cut his managerial teeth at Oldham Athletic, before joining the Blues as assistant to Billy McNeill. He knew that he faced a struggle for survival in his first campaign in charge of Manchester City and had the nous to make use of all available resources. Like Billy McNeill before him, Frizzell soon called upon the services of Ken Barnes:

"Some of the managers I worked for, gave the impression that they never listened to me or even read my reports. That was just the way it was. Most of them had their own people who they trusted and relied on and their first priority was bound to be the senior side, I suppose. But Frizz thought I had something to offer and asked me to look at players for the first team. I was delighted to do it, because I was getting a bit frustrated at the time, if I'm honest. We were still finding some good kids, even very good kids, despite all the problems and the chopping and changing at the club. But the board seemed determined to get what they could for them as soon as they showed the slightest promise. If I'm honest, it hurt a bit. I knew these lads had the talent to go on and have good careers, but they were moved on so fast, it made me wonder at times just what the bloody club was looking for. Some of the lads who moved on over a period of time, bugger me, like Earl Barrett, Paul Warhurst, Clive Wilson, Gerry Taggart, Steve Lomas, Chris Coleman, who's just taken over at Fulham as the youngest manager in the Premiership, Neil Lennon, John Beresford, Mike Milligan, Ashley Ward. They haven't done too fuckin' badly have they? Some of them moved on so early, that people don't even think them in connection with City, I suppose. But you always hope they'll remember where they got their first chance. I hope they do.

"Anyway, Frizz asked me to look at possible first team players. It was great, but a bit nerve wracking as well if I'm honest. I mean, you know that some of the kids will fall by the wayside, it's expected. But if you recommend a potential first teamer, especially if the club is strapped financially, he's expected to come up to the mark. I recommended Paul Stewart from Blackpool. I always thought he had something to offer; though, to be fair, he didn't stay too long after we were relegated. I also recommended Colin Hendry, who signed a bit later when Mel Machin was manager and Jimmy had gone as general manager, I think. In fairness to Frizz, he trusted me. When I suggested a player, he always said, 'That'll do for me Ken.' He might still have taken a look for himself, after all it was his name over the door when all was said and done, but he trusted me."

City were relegated at the end of the 86/87 season and the Chairman Peter Swales moved Jimmy Frizzell to general manager and installed Mel Machin from Norwich City as the new manager.

JIMMY FRIZZELL

Jimmy Frizzell first came up against Ken Barnes whilst playing for Oldham against Wrexham in the early 60s:

"Ken was Wrexham's player - manager at the time, maybe not quite as good as in his heyday, but still a hell of a player. I knew what I was good at and I knew I couldn't beat him for skill, so I took a fairly robust approach, shall we say. After a while, Ken got sick and tired of being kicked and just stopped dead in his tracks. I'll never forget it. He just turned me and said: 'Here, if you want the fuckin' ball that much, have it!' I didn't realise it at the time, but that was to be the start of a friendship that has lasted more than 40 years.

"At first we just met up when our paths crossed. I remember having a drink with him at Denis Law's 21st birthday do and later, when I was the manager at Oldham Athletic, I would see him at Boundary Park if he came to look at a player. We would always have a drink and a chat after the game. When we were together at City, well, that really cemented our friendship.

"Ken has an unbelievable passion for the game. He was always the first to volunteer to play in testimonials, even when he was old enough to know better. Even now, I'd say he thinks of himself, first and foremost, as a player. As well as a passion for the game, he has an amazing knowledge and a great eye for a player. When I was in charge at City, I could always trust his judgement. I told

him I needed a centre-forward and he came up with a young lad at Blackpool called Paul Stewart. He was just a raw kid, but Ken saw the potential in him and in light of what he went on to do, that wasn't a bad call was it? If there is, or has been, a better scout than Ken, I've never met him. First class, no doubt about it.

"As for the man, well, I'm sure anyone would tell you that Ken is incapable of hedging anything. Ask the question, you'll get a straight answer. Kit man or Chairman, it makes no difference to Ken. I'm sure his honesty has ruffled a few feathers, but I think the vast majority of people appreciated it. There was never any back-stabbing with him and if he respected you, there was no better man to have in your corner.

"Ken's office at City was a great place for ex-pros and football people. I think Peter Swales used to wonder what was going on in there sometimes, but I loved it. You were guaranteed a warm welcome and a cup of tea, whatever the time of day, and you never knew who you might meet in there.

"I also have to say that Ken has got a great sense of humour. Footballers never really grow up because they don't have to and most of them love the jokes and mickey taking that are part and parcel of any football club. Ken was no different but he could take a joke at his own expense and see the funny side of life. He always used to keep his papers in a little brief case and he took some stick about it, but he carried it with him everywhere he went. I remember he was done for driving over the limit and he was walking out of the police station after the doctor had confirmed the positive breathalyser reading. Ken was carrying his brief case as always and someone saw the case and, quite innocently, asked him if he was the doctor. Ken just looked at him and said, 'Am I the fuckin' doctor? The fuckin' doctor's just blown me out of the water!' Ken is one of the greats, as a player, a scout and as a man. A one off and a good man to have as a friend."

THE COACH

Mel Machin came in as team manager, with Jimmy Frizzell moving to the position of general manager, for the start of the 1987/88 campaign. He arrived from Norwich City with a reputation as a first class coach and in his two years at the helm, he took the club back into the top flight and achieved two of the most famous results in the club's history; the 10-1 win over Huddersfield and, of course, the 5-1 win over Manchester United in September 1989. Little more than 2 months after the win over the Reds, Machin was sacked by Chairman Peter Swales, following a poor run of results. Machin never really captured the hearts of the fans and Ken Barnes also found it hard to take to the new man:

"Bloody hell, he *was* a coach; steeped in the culture of coaching. He had code words for certain moves for fuck's sake! Honestly, he used names like Jack, Syd and Fred for them. I can't remember now exactly which name indicated which move, but it was for things like a reverse pass, a backheel or a stepover. I couldn't stop myself thinking back to the days when people did those things because they had been born with a gift. The vision, imagination and anticipation, not to mention the eyes up their arse, to know when to do these things. And you had to have the same qualities yourself to read their intentions or suffer the consequences. It was that old coaching bull, trying to break an art down into its constituent parts, so anyone can learn it.

"Of course, my antenna was straight up. He was another one, a bit like Malcolm I suppose, who thought having a good coach was more important than having good players. It used to drive me fuckin' crackers! He used to ask me to take a look at senior players, which was fair enough, but you never knew if he was listening to a word you were saying. I remember going into his office once and he was there with Frizz. Jimmy was on the phone and I started to talk to Mel about a player. When I finished, he just kept staring straight ahead and never answered me. Frizz was off the phone by now and looking at me and laughing. I turned to him and said 'What the fuck is this about?' He just smiled and shrugged. I think he'd got used to it! I walked out in the end and he still hadn't fuckin' answered me! He could be like that sometimes, away with the fairies.

"Machin threw in a lot of the kids and most of them survived and did okay, but I was always a bit wary. You have to be careful with youngsters and I couldn't help feeling sometimes, that it was the 'great coach' syndrome - wanting to prove he could take raw material and work miracles.

"The sad thing is that, once someone gets that steeped in coaching, they can become almost suspicious of natural talent. I recall my son, Peter, telling me about a conversation he'd had with Mel. Machin told Peter that he respected him as a pro, but that he didn't like wingers. That told me a lot.

"In fairness, his record at the club wasn't too bad. But there was a lot of talk of City being the type of set-up that needed a big name manager and he always struck me as the type of bloke who didn't particularly like the additional things that went with being a manager, as opposed to a coach. He never really seemed at ease with the media and whether you like it or not, by the end of the 80s that was very much part of the deal - especially at a club like City. The Chairman seemed to set great store by the big name thing, especially in terms of being a front man for the club. Well, that was never going to be Mel Machin.

"After the euphoria of beating United 5-1, I suppose the City fans got a bit carried away and were expecting things to take off from there. There were some good players coming through, but they were still just kids for the most part. It was a great day for the fans but, in retrospect, I'm not so sure the result did Mel

Machin too many favours, if you stand back and look at it. He was under pressure once the side started to struggle. If I'm being honest, I didn't lose any sleep about him going."

The "Big Name" arrived in December 1989. The man behind Everton's success in the 1980s, Howard Kendall.

THE BIG NAME

Howard Kendall came to Maine Road with a big reputation from his managerial success with Everton. After a playing career that had started with an FA Cup final appearance, aged 17, with Preston North End and peaked as part of an Everton midfield alongside Colin Harvey and World Cup winner Alan Ball, Kendall cut his managerial teeth at Blackburn, before putting together a formidable outfit at Goodison Park in the 1980s. Under his guidance the Toffees finally broke the domination of the English game by arch-rivals Liverpool. It was enough to make Howard Kendall a living legend to the blue half of Merseyside. He was a man inextricably linked with Everton - something Manchester City fans would become all too aware of before long. The side that Kendall built at Goodison was efficient rather than enthralling and they won plenty of trophies without stirring the blood of Ken Barnes:

"They were ratters really, weren't they? Effective certainly, but not always exciting to watch. Howard got the best out of them and they had a good spine with Southall, Radcliffe, Reidy and Graeme Sharpe, but they didn't get you on the edge of your seat, did they?

"The first thing Howard did, was to recreate what he'd done for Everton. He started to bring in lads who'd done a job for him there and, at the same time, he got rid of a few players the fans liked - Ian Bishop for example. Some of the supporters got a bit concerned. They wondered when it would stop; all these ex-Evertonians being drafted in. I could understand that to a certain extent. It's never easy to please everyone, of course.

"The fans want a manager to change things and build a successful side, but they still have their favourites and don't want to see them leave. Well, Howard didn't hang about as I recall. I have to say that, though I didn't necessarily agree with all his ideas, there was no doubt that Howard seemed to know what he was about. He had a plan and the record to back it up. On a personal level we got on alright. He was a good man and I'm sure, if things had worked out differently, he would have put together a useful side at Maine Road.

"He always used to tell me we had something in common, 'We never played for England Ken, but a lot of people thought we should have.' He was one of the managers who liked me to check on senior players for him as well as the youngsters. I used to enjoy it, but I'd never judge a player on one performance. I liked to watch them maybe half a dozen times - especially away from home. I think you can tell more about a laddie's character away from home. I never watched the ball, just the player. To be honest, the job was getting harder. I don't mean physically, but the game had changed and clubs seemed suspicious of anyone with real talent. They seemed to want players instilled with the idea of safety first. It used to discourage me to see the way that true talent was looked at as being almost dangerous. Take young Nicky Reid. When he first came to City, he had real talent. But most City fans will remember Nicky as a grafter and talk about his commitment. Of course, he did have those assets as well, but why did they have to grind the quality out of him? Nicky was more than just a grafter, a lot more - till the coaches got their hands on him.

"In the early days, I used to love going to lower league games. I always had that little feeling of excitement, that today might be the day. I was always hoping to find a bit of talent, a rough diamond if you like, with the potential to go on to higher levels. By the end of my time in the game, I used to find myself fuckin' off at half time, disheartened."

Less than a year after arriving at Maine Road, Kendall had left to return to Goodison, following the departure of Colin Harvey. Ken was amazed and made it clear that he thought Kendall was making the wrong decision:

"'Howard, what the fuck are you thinking about?'

'I know what you're saying Ken, but my heart's overruling my head.'

'Stuff that! Lightning doesn't strike twice in the same fuckin' place.'"

The rest, as they say, is history. Kendall did follow his heart, but failed to recreate his earlier glories at Everton and the man he'd brought to Maine Road as his on field General, Peter Reid, took up the reins as manager of Manchester City.

PART FIVE

OUT ON HIS EAR

When Peter Reid took over from Howard Kendall, it surprised Ken Barnes to a degree, but he was a popular choice with the supporters who had taken to Reid's committed style from the outset. As Kendall's captain during the glories days at Everton, Reid was better versed than most in the ideas and practices that had brought so much success to Goodison Park just a few short years before. He seemed an obvious, if inexperienced, successor to his mentor. The theory was borne out in reality as City finished 5th under Reid in season 90/91:

"Howard brought him in as a player, of course. He was getting on a bit, but he'd never been quick to start with, so losing a bit of pace was never going to be a problem. He seemed a decent enough lad and certainly you couldn't argue with his attitude out on the pitch. He was Howard's eyes and ears on the park. He was the ideal man really, to help establish what Kendall was trying to do. When Howard went back to Everton, Peter was, I suppose, the obvious choice, even if it was his first go at management. Having had the success he'd had at Everton under Kendall, at least you felt he'd carry on what Howard had started, rather than starting all over again from scratch. By then I think everyone, fans and players alike, were sick to death of all the chopping and changing."

Having enjoyed a successful time after taking over the reins from Howard Kendall, Peter Reid made some closed season changes to the backroom staff at the club. Those changes would include bringing an end to Ken Barnes' second spell at

Maine Road, after more than 20 years:

"Peter had had a good first season, no doubt about it. He'd brought in a few of his own people, which was fair enough and, as always, I just got on with my job. We had our differences of opinion, but that was normal. I remember a disagreement we had about Michael Hughes. I thought the lad was a real find, blessed with real talent, but Peter thought he was a bit of a "homer". We were never going to be close friends or anything like that. I didn't particular like the football, though you couldn't argue with the league position. But if I'm honest, I wasn't overly impressed with the people he brought in. It's just my opinion, of course, but take Sam Ellis for example. A couple of seasons earlier I'd recommended Colin Hendry to Jimmy Frizzell. I think Frizz took a look at the lad for himself but he trusted my judgement. I recall him saying that if I thought Hendry was good enough for Manchester City, that would do for him. Well, I'm at Maine Road under Peter Reid and one day Sam Ellis suddenly says to me :

'I don't think much of that centre-half. He's no good, he'll have to go'

'You fuckin' what? No good? He's better than you were, you ****. You were no fuckin' good!'

He looked at me, stunned, 'You don't sit on the fence do you?'

'No, I fuckin' don't!'

"Well they sold him anyway, but I can't help thinking he didn't do too badly for Blackburn and Scotland did he?

"Then one morning, Reid called me into his office and told me he wanted me to leave. I asked him if he was sacking me and he said he wasn't sacking me, but maybe it was time for me to leave - I'm not sure what the fuckin' difference is! He started waffling on about giving me a testimonial and then he asked me if I could do with a drink. He was a bit embarrassed, I think. I said, 'No thanks, but you look like you could do with one!' After that, I think I was on auto-pilot for a while. He never actually told me why he wanted me to leave and I never asked. Maybe he thought I was past it.

"I went to see Peter Swales about a pension. He offered me a testimonial and £20 a week. £20 a week, after more than 20 years! In the end we settled on £70.

"I left immediately, there was nothing else to do. I just walked out of Maine Road and went home and told my wife, June, I was out.

"I remember feeling quite calm at the time. I thought that, maybe, it was time to go and the job was certainly getting harder. I felt a bit helpless but also a bit resigned to it all. It didn't really hit me for a couple of days - I suppose it had all happened so fast - but then, bloody hell, it was like they'd cut my fuckin' legs off. I was walking round in a state of shock for a while, but I decided to keep away from the ground.

"I missed the involvement, because it had been such a big part of my life for so long. I still saw my old friends from the 50s, but I thought it best not to go to Maine Road. Then Tudor Thomas asked me to go to a game as his guest. I wasn't sure, but I decided to go in the end, for the chance to see some old friends. Well, I was having a drink in the Blue Room after the game, when one of the security lads came up to me looking very sheepish. I've never forgotten what he said:

'Excuse me, Mr Barnes, can I see your pass please?'

'Pass? A fuckin' pass? After 40 years at the club, I need a pass to come in here?'

'You can't come in the Blue Room without a pass.'

"Fuckin' hell, I was livid. The order had obviously come from on high, but I really couldn't believe they would treat me like that after 40 years. It's not as if I'd kicked up a fuss or anything and I'd hardly walked away with a big pay off. It just seemed so petty. It wasn't as if I'd done a bad job over the years was it? I really thought that was me finished with Manchester City for good. I can't find the words to tell you how I felt at that moment, I really can't."

Ken Barnes may well have thought that he'd made his last ever visit to Maine Road, but in football, as in life, what goes around eventually comes around. Within 2 years the manager and the Chairman had gone and Ken Barnes was back at Manchester City, as a part time scout under Brian Horton.

TESTIMONIALS

When Ken Barnes was sacked (or advised to retire!) by Peter Reid, he had served Manchester City, over two periods, for more than 30 years. He was promised a testimonial in return for over 20 years in coaching and scouting roles at the club, since rejoining the fold at the request of Joe Mercer. The testimonial was to be an additional recognition of his contribution to the cause, to go with his pension of £70 per week. It was, in fact, Ken's second testimonial. The first was awarded for his ten years as a player at Maine Road.

The first game, against Don Revie's International All Stars Eleven, took place on the 28th April 1975, and the visitors included such notables as Bobby Charlton, Denis Law, George Best, Gordon Banks, Frank McLintock and Malcolm McDonald. The referee was no less a personage than Jack Taylor. There was also a showbiz 7-a-side game, in which the guest list included Bob Greaves, David Lloyd, Harry Pilling, Clive Lloyd, Gareth Edwards, Alex Murphy, Bernard Manning, George Roper, Jimmy Tarbuck and Bobby Johnstone.

Despite the highly impressive turn out, Ken doesn't remember too much about the game, other than that it all seemed to happen very quickly:

"It all happened in a bit of a rush, as I remember. Still, it was very nice to see all those famous faces turn out for me."

Ken's second testimonial match was played on Friday 8th May 1992 at Maine Road, with Alex Ferguson's Manchester United providing the opposition. The game had been arranged by the Testimonial Committee, made up of Tudor Thomas, John Doherty, Denis Law, Colin Barlow and Joe Richardson. The match was refereed by the late, great, Neil Midgley.

Although Alex Ferguson brought his full first team squad, very poor weather meant that, sadly, there was to be no bumper crowd for Ken, though he did receive enough to pay of the small balance of his mortgage and get a new car. Not quite the six or seven figure sums generated nowadays, but Ken was very grateful and also appreciative of the comments of his peers in the match programme.

One of the game's all time greats, Tom Finney said of Ken, "he was a stylish and cultured player of great ability and a very nice fellow."

Billy Wright, who won over a hundred England caps, described him as, "A true professional and a credit to the game."

Nat Lofthouse, the 'Lion of Vienna', spoke of Ken playing with "cultured confidence."

The ever pragmatic Alex Ferguson had this to say, "I'm glad he's retiring, because it means we can get him out of our hair. He's been a wonderful servant for City as a player and a valuable member of the backroom staff. We at United have always been aware of his presence in the scouting area. You only have to look at the players who have come through his staff, to realise his great knowledge of the game."

Ken has a lot of time for Alex Ferguson:

"A great, great manager. Look at his record and as for understanding what makes people tick, he's second to none. I was over at United's place in Carrington a while back and got talking to Alex about the game. Roy Keane and David Beckham were walking past and he called them over and introduced me to them. He told them that if they played till they were a hundred, they still wouldn't be able to pass a ball like I could. I'm not daft, he probably said it to make an old man happy. Well I can tell you Alex, it did."

To be given two testimonials pays eloquent tribute to the contribution of Ken Barnes to Manchester City in whatever role. The Chairman of the Testimonial Committee, Tudor Thomas, described Ken as, "A loyal servant, whose honesty, knowledge of the game and respect for others have been largely responsible for the success of the club's youth policy."

TUDOR THOMAS

Honorary President, Tudor Thomas, has been a keen fan of Manchester City since the early 50s and a friend of Ken Barnes for over 30 years. He still refers to him, simply, as 'The Right-half', convinced that Ken's performances for the Blues defined the role. He still relishes his memories of the City side of the 50s and has no doubt about the pivotal part played by Ken:

"He was a magnificent player. You could catalogue all the things he wasn't good at and still end up with the shrewdest football mind I've ever seen. When I think back to the Revie Plan, I have to smile. Don't get me wrong, Don Revie was a great player but, to my mind at least, it was Ken who made the plan work. There were some great players in that side, but he was the brain."

Tudor and Ken became friends in the 70s and Tudor was on the organising committee for Ken's second testimonial in the early 90s.

"It was a privilege to be involved and the least I could do when you think of his immense contribution to the club. I helped organise a game with Manchester United. Alex Ferguson was fantastic, he insisted on bringing his best team. From a financial point of view, Leeds winning the title that year was a disaster.

I reckon it cost Ken £100,000. If United had been champions, they'd have brought 10,000 with them to the game. In the event, there were about 300."

Tudor makes no secret of his respect and admiration for Ken:

"You don't have to do much for someone to call you a 'legend' these days but Ken is exactly that. I've never heard anyone say a bad word about him, although I'm sure there must be the odd director who might argue with me on that point. It's no secret that Ken and directors didn't mix. I can remember the Chairman, Peter Swales, looking in the door of Ken's office at Maine Road once. He was looking for someone and Ken just told him straight, 'There's no point you coming in here, you know fuck all about football...' Exit Peter Swales.

"The talent he found for the club was staggering really. Don't forget either, that he signed the lads when the club was in turmoil really. He was brilliant with the youngsters and their parents. He never used to go overboard about the boys, no matter how talented they were. Even when he signed an absolute gem, such as Paul Lake, you always got the same answer if you asked about them, 'The boy's got a chance.'

"The kids he signed were all in awe of him. They all called him Mr Barnes, never Ken. I can remember when David White got called up for England. He was understandably delighted and said: "What do you think about that, Ken?" One look from Ken, along with a reminder not to let the call up go to his head, and it was back to Mr Barnes in very short order, I can tell you.

"Ken Barnes is part of the very fabric of Manchester City. It's impossible to put a value of what he's done for this club over 50 years. It was great to watch him play and it's been great to enjoy his friendship. He's a true Manchester City legend is 'The Right-half.'"

BACK TO THE BLUES II

The start of the 1993/1994 season was to prove momentous, even by City's standards. Peter Swales was under growing pressure from the disgruntled fans after the Blues had finished the previous season in a lacklustre 9th place. Meanwhile, arch rivals United had taken the first-ever Premiership title in style, winning by a clear 10 points.

Former journalist John Maddock had come in as general manager at Maine Road. Maddock was adamant that he was his own man, rather than a mouthpiece for Peter Swales, but the popular belief was that his role was to play hatchet man, following rumours of a rift between the Chairman and the Manager. Just four games into the new campaign, the Peter Reid era was over. As City fans waited on a big name replacement for the sacked scouser, Maddock unveiled the latest occupant of English football's hottest managerial seat - the virtually unknown Brian Horton.

Horton had been recruited from Oxford United and would go on to win over large numbers of City fans with his honesty and desire to play open, attractive football. At the time though, his appointment was taken as incontrovertible proof of the club's decline.

The groundswell of support for City legend turned successful businessman, Francis Lee, as replacement Chairman, increased the growing pressure on the beleaguered Peter Swales and in November, after 20 years in charge, he resigned.

Francis Lee finally assumed control in February 1994 and one of his first moves was to bring Ken Barnes back into the Maine Road fold. Ken returned in a part-time scouting capacity and would continue in that role for a further 6 years. Ken had not been back to the club since the incident in the Blue Room, but any residual bitterness or ill-feeling was aimed at the previous regime and the pull of the Blues drew him back:

"I never thought I'd go back after what had happened, but it had all changed of course. I had no argument with the people in charge now, so I was pleased to be asked to go back and to get the chance to help. Let's face it, there was so much going on, the club could have gone into freefall. Jimmy Frizzell was chief scout and he told them to get me back. If I'm honest, I'd missed it - the day-to-day involvement with the game that is, not the politics obviously. I'd never have gone back unless things had changed though, not with the previous lot - no way.

"I really liked Brian Horton. He was a really good lad who wanted to play football the way I liked to see it played. He was dead straight and he wanted so much to do well at City. He'd learnt his trade at a small club and now he had the chance to make his mark in the top flight, even if the odds were against him. He was desperate to be a success at Maine Road. Let's face it, it was never going to be easy for him, was it? Unless he won something, and quick, he was always going to be tainted by association with the previous regime. He was the last throw of the dice by the previous Chairman and he was always going to be tarred with the same brush. I really liked him and in fairness to the City fans, they have come to appreciate him more since he left the club. I'm glad about that, he's a good football man."

Despite his best efforts, Horton was sacked at the end of his second season in charge, as City finished 17th in the Premier Division. If Horton's appointment had caused controversy, his successor would provoke an even stronger reaction.

Blues fans had, as usual, been expecting a big name replacement for Horton and were, consequently, decidedly underwhelmed when Alan Ball took over. Ball's record as a player was exemplary; success at club level with Everton and Arsenal and a fine international career, including a World Cup winners medal in 1966. As a manager, the story had been rather less impressive. He took over at Maine Road in time for the start of the 1995/96 season.

BALL AND THE GEORGIAN GENIUS

The short period under Alan Ball saw Manchester City relegated at the end of his first season in charge. Ball had an uneasy, albeit interesting, relationship with the Blues fans and the media. Moreover, there were rumours of a confrontational style of management, involving much comparison of his own qualities and achievements as a player with those of his current charges. Other than relegation he will, probably, be best remembered as the man who introduced Georgi Kinkladze, the massively gifted Georgian, to the City team. Ken Barnes remembers Ball as an interesting character:

"He'd had a great career as a player, no doubt about it. He had a good engine, could pass a good ball, had a little bit of vision. He certainly had tenacity and made the most of what he had. But his record as a manager wasn't up to much. I suppose, if I'm honest, I was a bit surprised when he got the job. But it wasn't down to me, so I just got on with my own work. I know a lot of fans think he got the job because him and Franny went back a long way. It was in the papers at the time, as I recall, about the old pals act, especially after City had been linked with some more obvious and successful names to take over. Funnily enough, I don't think Alan Ball and Franny were that close at all. You'd have to ask Franny, of course, but I got the impression that maybe he did have other managers in mind, but had to think again when he found out how much it would cost to get them to Maine Road. I think it was more a case of needs must, rather than any old pals act.

"One thing about Alan, he loved to talk about the game. We

used to sit and talk sometimes at Platt Lane and at Maine Road and we didn't always see eye-to-eye. He has things he believes in and so do I. Sometimes, he used to get a bit of a bee in his bonnet about things, but he did love to talk about football and that suited me down to the ground.

"I can remember when he was getting ready to sell Steve Lomas to West Ham. He insisted that Steve was just a worker. I told him that when Steve Lomas came to City he had plenty of talent - it had just been fuckin' coached out of him!"

As for Georgi Kinkladze, the fans loved him, but the experts sometimes seemed divided about his qualities. Perhaps more than any other City player since Rodney Marsh, Kinkladze provoked comment from pundits and punters alike. For Ken Barnes, the Georgian maestro has no case to answer:

"Brilliant, a marvellous player. Amazing feet, balance, pace, could lick people and a real football brain. Wonderful vision. There's no comparison with Rodney Marsh. Rodney was gifted, he had talent, but crucially, in my opinion, he lacked the football savvy to use his talent in the best interests of the team. Without that, you're just a tupenny ha'penny ball player, a circus act. Kinkladze had the talent and the brains. It still amazes me that one of the teams trying to close the gap on United didn't try to get him. You only saw glimpses of what he could do at City, because no matter how good you are, you need good players around you. If you'd put him in the United team at the time, fuckin' hell - they would have won everything including the Grand National. In some ways, it's sad that we haven't had the chance to see him on a stage to do justice to his talent. I really think he would have been one of the greats of his day. It tells you a lot about how the game is going, that no one did give him the chance; too talented to be trusted, I suppose. Alright, he went to Ajax and Derby, but he could have been an absolute catalyst at a top club. He could have had a bigger part to play than Cantona did for United. In fact, given a chance at

Old Trafford, he could have had more of an impact than Cantona did. I really believe that. Alex took a chance on Cantona and got repaid in spades. If someone had given Georgi the same sort of chance, who knows what he might have done for them?

"In my opinion, he really was a special talent. He just never got the right opportunity or stage to prove it. For me that's a real shame, it truly is."

Alan Ball left Maine Road before the end of August 1996.

FREEFALL

Following the departure of Alan Ball, Manchester City went perilously close to freefall, before Joe Royle began the long haul back to the Premiership from Division 2 of the Nationwide League. The intervening period was one observed with something approaching horror by Ken Barnes:

"Fuckin' hell - they were desperate times. I could hardly believe what was going on at times. Alan Ball left, Asa held the fort for a bit as I recall, then Steve Coppell was here for 2 minutes and then he was gone. Phil Neal as caretaker, in and out in a matter of weeks. I hardly had the chance to meet them, let alone get to know them.

"At times like that, you can only hope that the senior pros will show the character to hold the club together. In fairness, everything seemed to be falling apart so quickly, I really thought the club could go under. When Frank Clark came in, he seemed to steady things for a bit, before it started to go downhill again. I can only speak from my personal experience, but Frank surrounded himself with his own little group, which a lot of new managers do of course. I got the impression that he wanted nothing to do with the people who were already at the club when he arrived. I often used to sit and talk football with

Frizz at Platt Lane but Clark never came and spoke to us. He preferred to stick with the company of his assistants, Alan Hill and Richard Money. I never had any significant dealings with him personally, so it's hard for me to judge him.

"Nevertheless, there's a bit of me that can't help thinking that, if you're in the kind of trouble City were at the time, you need to look at all the strengths and weaknesses at the club. You don't ignore what is there already, just because it was there before you were. I'm not saying we had any kind of magic wand, far from it, but Frizz and me knew a lot about the club and a fair bit about the game. Let me make something absolutely clear; I'm not talking about interfering. He was the manager after all, but I wanted to help in any way I could. This had been my club for nearly 50 years for God's sake. I would have thought that picking a few brains would have been worth the effort. Even if he decided, after speaking to us, that we were talking through our arses!"

Under Clark, City finished 14th in Division 1 of the Nationwide League. The following season, in February 1998, Clark was sacked along with his backroom staff, as the Blues found themselves in the bottom two. Francis Lee's tenure as Chairman ended the following month. Ken had mixed feeling about the two departures:

"I felt sorry for Franny. After what he'd achieved as a player, I think the fans were expecting him to solve all the problems at Maine Road at a stroke. Sadly, life doesn't work like that, does it? Franny Lee riding to the rescue. It's a wonderful idea and I think the vast majority of people hoped it would all come right under him. It would have been a fairy tale, but they only come true in books. As for Frank Clark, well, I didn't really have any dealings with him, as I said before. If he had asked me about players to bring to City, there's one thing I could have told him for definite - 'for fuck's sake don't waste three million on Lee Bradbury!' Like I said, I didn't get to know the man; but that signing told me a lot about the manager."

Clark was replaced by former City striker Joe Royle. Royle had been linked with the manager's job at Maine Road before, but finally took up the reins with the club deep in relegation trouble. He failed to stop the rot and at the end of the 97/98 season the Blues tumbled into Division 2 of the Nationwide League.

END OF THE CITY ROAD

As Joe Royle began the process of restoring Manchester City to former glories, Ken Barnes found himself a casualty of the new regime. The notional reason for his sacking was that his services were too expensive. At this point, Ken was being paid £100 per week by the club as a part time scout:

"I took it a lot better than I did being sacked by Peter Reid. Don't get me wrong, it still hurt, of course it did. But I was getting on a bit, though I certainly didn't see myself as senile. I told Joe I wasn't responsible for some of the recent signings! But it was different this time round; I felt I'd done my stint. I'd made a contribution, both as a player and in terms of the talent I'd signed for the club. I'd had a good innings, if you like. As for Joe, I got on with him okay. If I bump into him, we always have a chat. He's always very pleasant and affable. I must say though, that I always thought there was much more to Joe than his public image of genial Joe Royle. I always thought that he chose to show that side, but maybe he was a much more complex man than that. I may be wrong, but that was always my impression.

"I have always got on with Willie Donachie. He's dead straight. We've had a few arguments though. One of the last ones was over this thing you see, where all the players gather on one side of the pitch for a goal kick. 20 players in about 30 square yards. I couldn't believe what was happening:

'Hey, Willie,' I said, 'what the fuck is that about? Why don't you get someone out on the other side?'

'You know how it is Ken, they won't listen. They don't want to take the responsibility.'

'They won't fuckin' listen? Make 'em listen. You're the fuckin' coach.'

"That's football for you, 80 odd years experience between us and we still end up arguing. Everyone always thinks he's right - it's the nature of the game and the people in it. Willie is a real football man though. I suppose we're all still players at heart, but he worked harder at it than most. He kept himself incredibly fit. Unless I'm mistaken, I think he played for the reserves when he was about 50. It was supposed to be a one-off, but you never know with Willie!"

Ken Barnes' 50 year professional association with Manchester City is now over, although his love for the Blues endures. On most match days, Ken is to be found at the ground, talking football with his trademark honesty and passion. He can often be found discussing the game with former team mates, Paddy Fagan and Johnny Williamson. As they talk, the years fall away and they speak as players rather than ex players. As Paddy so aptly describes it: "We've never had a bad game since we turned 70!"

If you are fortunate enough to have the opportunity to observe this post-game ritual, you will soon realise that this is not just a chance for old players to lament the passing of the game's better days. Footballers, of all generations, (though probably not too many directors) make a beeline for Ken and it is obvious, to even the most casual of onlookers, that this is a man held in the highest esteem by his peers. When he talks about the game, people listen and with good reason.

Football is still a consuming passion for Ken. His time in the game has left him with strong beliefs about the sport he loves.

As you would expect of a man steeped in football for so long, he has his hopes and fears for the future of the game and his concerns about the people shaping the sport:

"I really liked Kevin Keegan. I liked him a lot and he wanted to play the game the way I believe it should be played. I think it's a shame that things didn't work out for him. I wish him well. I enjoyed some of the football played under him. Players like Ali Benarbia and Eyal Berkovic have kept us on the edge of our seats in recent times, but there aren't many of them about. He must have been delighted at the way young Shaun Wright-Phillips blossomed as a player. Shaun has so much promise. A couple of years ago, when everyone first began to take notice and talk about him, I didn't say much, because it's a very important point in a youngster's career. You hope they don't start to believe all the hype and lose a bit of focus. I'm delighted to say that he seems to have ignored all the bull and has just tried to get better and better as a player. If he keeps working and learning, he'll be something a bit special. It's great to watch a real talent develop. Whenever you heard Kevin talk about the lad, you could tell how excited he was about Shaun, and rightly so. I hope the boy goes on to be all he can be, I really do.

"I was sorry to see Kevin leave, but it was on the cards. He seemed to have lost a bit of his sparkle towards the end. I don't know much about Stuart Pearce, but he's made a very promising start. My son, Peter, played with him at Coventry for a while and thinks highly of him. The first full season in charge will be the real test of course. But he's certainly started well and has made a great early impression. He certainly knows his own mind and talks a lot of sense. I really hope he thrives at City and the club thrives under him.

"Sadly of course, for every Kevin Keegan or Stuart Pearce, there's a Howard Wilkinson. I know what people will say; Wilkinson won the League with Leeds, whereas Kevin lost out with Newcastle, but fuckin' hell, what a load of shite he talks! He brought a book out a bit back, I borrowed it off Jimmy Frizzell - what a load of bollocks it was.

"It's when I listen to Wilkinson and his sort that I despair. He's part of that culture that takes a simple game and tries to dress it up in bollocks and bullshit. They want to make everything so technical, when the only real question to be asked is this; can the lad play? If he has that one talent, it really is a simple game.

"The club structure, nowadays, amazes me. I'm not saying I'd want to go back to how things were when I was starting out - no fuckin' way - that was a very hard world. But tell me this, every club has a dietician and a psychologist these days - can they put a football brain in your head? Can they bollocks. Of course, all the people at The FA, and the boards of directors at the big clubs, are dazzled with these new fangled ideas. But it's not worth a carrot, if you can't find lads with the ability to play the game. Everyone seems to be looking for new ideas. I remember Joe Royle working with the players and they were running with back packs on. I was a bit intrigued, I must admit. I stopped to watched for a bit, assuming there must be weights in the packs. All of a sudden, a fuckin' parachute pops out of the back pack. Joe said it was all about drag and resistance to improve muscle strength. He asked me what I thought. I said very impressive Joe, but I used to do it by running with Dave Ewing on my back. Fuckin' parachutes! I bet they paid a bloody fortune for them. No doubt it impressed some director or other. In my opinion, worrying about diets and stuff is fine, if all the basics are in place. If the big picture is right, I don't mind a bit of tinkering round the edges for that little bit extra, but I can't help thinking there's a lot more important things to get sorted before pasta or parachutes.

"People have bought into the hype. The game is marketed so well; every game is supposed to be fantastic. Well, I'm telling you, that's bollocks. All the top modern players are described as 'Greats of the Game'. I don't think so. Look at David Beckham - he's a global superstar, but it's all marketing. Oh, the laddie can play, make no mistake. He's an excellent passer and strikes a good dead ball, but he can't tackle or lick people and doesn't score many goals from open play. Are you trying to tell me he's a better midfield player than Colin Bell was? Or a better wide man, on the right, than Mike Summerbee? Not a chance. To hear people talk, you would think he was fuckin' Superman. It's the way of the world nowadays; everything is hyped up, to the point where reality starts to bloody blur. Ordinary players are touted as extraordinary. Well I'm not buying that. The only player, in the last decade, I would see as having all the qualities of a great player is Paul Gascoigne and that was because he had too much talent for it to be coached out of him.

"You've only got to look at the England team of the past 15 or 20 years. Greats? Who for fuck's sake? Take Bryan Robson, for example. Now, Bryan is a lovely fellah and by the standards of the modern game he's a giant. He was very good at all elements of the game and an absolute cornerstone of the team. But surely, if you're looking for that special quality, that something extra at international level, you use a player like Bryan to provide a platform. A platform for someone with something a bit special to offer. Glenn Hoddle had a wonderful football brain, real vision. Surely, in that case, you use Bryan's all round game to allow Hoddle to work his magic. Bryan could get a stranglehold on the midfield and then Glenn could add the craft to provide the attacking threat. We'll never know now, but I believe that their respective talents, used properly, could have really provided a potent midfield combination. What actually happened? They tried to turn Hoddle into a hard running, back tracking, midfielder. Why? We had fuckin' loads of them. We're talking about the national side for God's sake, and Carlton Palmer's winning England caps? Fuck me!

"I have to be careful, otherwise it just sounds like an old has-been moaning about the modern game. But there are things which concern me, especially the overemphasis on coaching and the lack of real flair and talent. Imagination and improvisation seem to be dirty words these days; talent is looked at with suspicion rather than appreciation. That depresses me, it really does.

"When I hear people going on about how the players of the past couldn't survive in the modern game, I have to bite my lip. Are you trying to tell me that Alfredo di Stefano couldn't play nowadays? Or Tom Finney? Fuck off. Di Stefano was the best I ever saw. He had it all; craft, control, pace together with a wonderful football brain. He was the most complete footballer I ever saw, and they want to tell me he'd struggle in the Premiership - bollocks. Good players could play in any era. Di Stefano would be a star today and Gascoigne would have been great in the 50s, no doubt about it."

As he looks back over a 50-year involvement in professional football, Ken has reached a stage in his life when it is understandable for him to take stock of his career in the game. He covers his ideas and beliefs on key areas of professional football later in the book, but he looks back on his own time, especially as a player, with few regrets. He grew up in an age when aspiring footballers were expected to take responsibility for their decisions and actions. As a consequence, he is less inclined to bemoan the things that didn't quite work out for him, because he chose the path he took, nobody else:

"No regrets really. It would have been nice to play for England, but it never happened, so I never worried about it. Some people have said I was a bit too outspoken for the Establishment. If that was the case and it did cost me the chance of a full England cap, then so be it. I was true to myself and what I believed in, and I think that's important - it certainly is to me. I got to captain the England 'B' team and the Football League side and, don't forget, I played in 2 FA Cup finals at Wembley. Fuckin' hell, there are hundreds of great players who can't say that.

"Still, I'm glad I played when I did, because I was a creative player. I wasn't much of a defender or a tackler, but I like to think that if I got the ball something might happen. I don't think modern coaches would like me too much - I might be a bit too adventurous for them. I didn't play safe all the time. The money would have been nice, though it's gone a bit daft now. We were like slaves compared to the modern lads. Still, I sometimes think we enjoyed ourselves more than they seem to.

"Nothing compares to playing, but to get the chance to come back and be part of Manchester City for another 30 years was wonderful. I like to think I got on with most of the managers I worked for, but I especially liked Joe Mercer, Tony Book, John Bond, Billy McNeill and Jimmy Frizz. They were all genuine blokes who knew the game and you could always have a laugh with them. Away from City, I liked Sir Matt Busby at Manchester United and Shanks at Liverpool. Bill was football daft. Bloody hell, now he did eat, drink and sleep the game. What a character. I've also got a lot of time for Sir Alex Ferguson. He has done a fantastic job at United. He has a truly great knowledge of football and footballers and what a will to win. He's a great lad, but I'm not sure I'd like to be a reporter covering United. He's not a big fan of the media Alex, is he?"

Ken Barnes says he doesn't miss the game as much as he thought he might:

"I missed the the involvement at first, but I was getting older and the talent was getting scarcer. You do get to a point, where you don't stop caring, but you do feel it's up to someone else to take up the fight. I'll always follow the game, of course, and especially City, but I've had my time now. I've still got all that

I've learned over 50 years tucked away in my head and if someone wants to ask me what I think, I'll always tell them, but the day to day stuff is over for me now."

Nevertheless, having spent time in his company, as we've worked on this book, I get the feeling that a request to run the rule over a player might still get a sympathetic hearing from the man.

Football has been central to Ken's life and he still talks about the game with the passion you only ever find in the truly committed. He has his concerns about the game. But they are the concerns of a man who wants to see his chosen sport striving to attain new heights. He is convinced that it will only do that by addressing its weaknesses, rather than hiding behind a media induced myth, that the game has reached some kind of footballing El Dorado.

NOT OVER YET

Although Ken's 50 year association with Manchester City has ended, the game of football continues to exert its influence on him. Over recent years, he has enjoyed a growing involvement with grass roots football in Malaysia. Ken's daughter, Karen, has lived in Malaysia since the mid 1980s and along with her business partner, Subramaniam Palandaram, she was becoming increasingly concerned about the lack of football opportunities for the country's young people.

Karen enlisted the knowledge and expertise of her dad to help launch Ken Barnes Soccer Skills. Ken, as usual, found himself involved more by accident than by design:

"We started going over about 10 years ago for a holiday and to see Karen. I could see that Karen and Subra were very keen to make things happen. Subra is mad about Liverpool, but he was always telling me that there was nothing in Malaysia for the kids who loved football, especially the poor kids. When people start to ask for a bit of advice, you get drawn in, don't you? They asked me questions and I asked a few questions back. It started to appeal to me, because it was like starting at the ground up. Having spent so much time telling everyone that coaching was killing the game in this country, I had a chance to get involved in a place where the coaches hadn't taken over yet. I had the chance to put my beliefs into practice."

The official launch came in February 2000, after testing the water in late 1999 with soccer schools in the Klang Valley. The basic premise was to provide a community service to improve the standards of the game in Malaysia and also to look for talented kids, who might possess the talent to go further in the sport.

Karen took Soccer Skills on the road nationwide and it was a chance for Ken to test his long-held belief that the kids would acquire the basics of the game more readily in a more relaxed and less structured environment. He wanted to avoid, if at all possible, the highly organised formats that prevail in the UK. There were 20 tournaments in the 2001/2002 season, across all the states of the Malaysian Peninsular. On average, each tournament included 500 boys between the ages of 10 and 16.

Learning lessons as they go, Soccer Skills have devised a new game called Footskills. As a 5-a-side game, it requires no special facilities and allows Soccer Skills to arrange a tournament in just about any location. The games are 5 minutes each way, to allow the greatest number of boys the chance to play. Boys with real talent can move on to regional and central trials with Ken himself; the ultimate objective being to join The Ken Barnes Soccer Skills Academy in Kangar, Perlis. From there, Ken hopes to channel lads with professional potential to England. The hope is to develop a two-way street of opportunity, with the chance for Malaysian footballers to play in England and for those with the football expertise in this country, to take a growing involvement with the game there.

Once boys reach the Academy, the coaching is guided by Ken and is based on his beliefs about how the game should be played, learned and taught.

Over the first 2 years of its existence, over 10,000 boys passed through the football tournaments and because it is Ken's strong belief that money should not be a factor and that a lack of funds should not spoil a boy's chances, all the tournaments are free of charge. Ken was adamant that every kid should have the opportunity, at least, to show what they could do:

"I didn't want anyone to miss out. Remember, when we were kids we had next to nothing. But some of these kids, especially in the rural areas, have literally nothing. Karen did really well with sponsors, so they could give everyone a go. Once the kids started to progress through the trials to the Academy, I told the coaches what I wanted in no uncertain terms. Let them play, give advice not orders and instil the idea that practice makes perfect. I picked the coaches I trusted. I wasn't bothered about badges, just the right attitude to the game. Funnily enough, Karen told me that the football authorities contacted her recently, expressing concern that the Academy coaches didn't have the highest level of badges. She told them straight: 'If all your coaches with the highest level badges are so good, how come Malaysia is so bad at football?'

"I was proud of her for that. I told her to let the Academy coaches get the badge, if it saved a lot of hassle, because I would tell them to forget all the shite they'd heard once they got back to the Academy."

In football, as in life, it does no harm to have influential friends and since June 2002 Ken Barnes Soccer Skills has had a royal patron. His Royal Highness Prince Syed Faizuddin Putra ibni Tuanka Syed Sirajuddin - Prince Regent of Perlis (the son of the present King of Malaysia) has been an enthusiastic backer of the Academy and the scheme. He also helped in efforts to set up a schools football league in Perlis, which started in February 2003. The scheme is also supported by the National Sports Council.

As the scheme starts to produce players, three boys have already been to England for trials and assessment at Birmingham City. The initials reports suggest that the boys have the requisite skill but need to work on their physical strength. Ken is under no illusions that it will be easy for Malaysian players in this country:

"It's not just the football, there's a massive culture shock to be overcome as well, but we've made a start. The signs are promising that the basic talent is there, we can always work on the physical side of things. I'm pleased about the scheme to get football into the schools. I've said it before, but one of the things that I found really disheartening about the game in Manchester was that fewer and fewer schools were playing football. Two hundred had packed in altogether. Well, with a lot of work from Karen and Subra, and with the help of the Prince, things are going the other way in Malalysia and that's got to be good news for the game there, it really has."

Ken's time in the professional game in England may now be over. But this involvement with the game half way round the world has allowed him to maintain his hands-on contact with the sport he loves. It has also allowed the sport in Malaysia to call upon the services of a man of immense football knowledge. After the dramatic impact of the scheme, Ken is now one of the best known names in Malaysian football and he gets to rub shoulders with royalty:

"The Prince is a great character. He loves his football. His favourite player is Bryan Robson, so I got Bryan to sign a picture for him. The Prince was well pleased, I can tell you. My wife June and me got invited to the Royal Palace for a dinner party with the Prince. One of his equerries, or some such, phoned us up to tell us what we should wear. We took it all on board and got ourselves ready. We got to the Palace, done up to the nines. We got shown into the room to meet the Prince and he's there with a bloody football shirt on! He's been an unbelievable source of support though. He loves his football and has made a terrific contribution to what Karen and Subra and everyone is trying to do."

Like most things in his football career, Ken found himself involved in his latest venture by chance, rather than by planning a grand entrance. It will be truly exciting to see how this opportunity to put his football credo into practice, impacts on the game in Malaysia over the years to come.

BECAUSE BULLSHIT BAFFLES BRAINS

One thing guaranteed to cause the Barnes hackles to rise is the subject of coaching. Ken believes, with a passion, that the modern cult of coaching is largely the recourse of charlatans. He rails against the idea that anyone with the capacity to earn a few badges can pass on the secrets of football to anyone with the desire to learn. The notion that the game is a science, that can be broken down into its constituents parts and then imparted to willing pupils, is viewed with jaundice. At its irreducible core, he believes that football is an art not a science. The best players are born with a gift to be coaxed, not coached, to fulfilment:

"Don't you think it's funny how all the best coaches work with the best players. Who taught George Best to play? Or Len Shackleton? Or Colin Bell? Nobody taught them, because you cannot teach what they had. Good players are born with the ability to play. They have to hone their skills and good young players can learn from experienced players but there is not a coach in the world who can turn a poor player into a good player, I don't care how many fuckin' badges he's got. But the belief, nowadays, is that the coach can fix it. Players wait to be told what to do and how to do it. All that does, is to breed players who don't want to take responsibility for their actions on the pitch. Think about it for a minute - coaches concentrate on the coachable; safety first, keep it simple, play the way you're facing etc - but what about encouraging people to try something different? The little bit of magic that can change a game. They can't coach that, so, to justify their existence, they discourage it. Kids end up getting bollocked for trying the things that made them good players in the first place. Good players make it, nowadays, despite coaching, not because of it.

"It's not just a modern thing. You can go back to the 50s and Walter Winterbottom. He was one of the people who really started the mania for coaching. He was a bloody school teacher for God's sake. England lost to a foreign country for the first time and suddenly it was panic stations. The nation that had given football to the world had lost a match. What did they expect? Did they really think the other countries wouldn't improve? That didn't mean there was anything wrong with our game. That Hungarian side of the early 50s was exceptional. They should have won the World Cup in 1954. What have they won since? Not even a bowl of soup. But the genie was out of the bottle. Coaching would be the answer.

"All the fuss when England won the World Cup in 1966. The 'Wingless Wonders' and all that shite. It was hailed as a great era for English football, but why? If you look back, the host nation nearly always does well in the World Cup, look at Sweden in 1958 for God's sake. Remember as well, England never played a game away from Wembley. I don't want to do the lads who won the Cup any disserve, but do you really believe they would have won it in Italy or South America? For my money, there were only two truly great players in that team

- Bobby Charlton and Gordon Banks. I know people will make claims for some of the others, especially Bobby Moore, but, in my view, the rest were good players, not great players. Bobby found his perfect niche as a twin centre back. For someone with a half decent football brain, and Bobby certainly had that, it's an easy position to play, because it's all in front of you. I'm not convinced he would have been half as successful as a wing-half or as a midfielder. Suddenly, Alf Ramsey is hailed as a master coach and tactician and 'winger' has become a dirty word. It's like they're all searching for the magic wand, to solve all the football situations you can be faced with in a game. I'm not sure they'll ever find the answer they're looking for, but if they do, I'm pretty sure it will involve good players rather than a bloody coach.

"If you look at the great managers of the modern era, say, from the 60s onwards, I think you can learn something important. Don't you think it's strange that the most successful managers of that period didn't have any sort of reputation as coaches? Matt Busby, Joe Mercer, Jock Stein, Bill Shankly, Bob Paisley, Brian Clough and Alex Ferguson. What did they have in common? It certainly wasn't a belief in the magic of coaching, I can tell you that. Liverpool never even had a coach for fuck's sake. I remember once, I'd been sounding off about the negative impact of coaching and I was talking to Bob Paisley. He was agreeing with me and I asked him outright:

'Look Bob, you're in the best position of anyone to tell people what you think about coaching. Liverpool are winning everything in sight and you've not even got a coach. You've got the perfect platform, they'll have to listen to you.'

"Bob just looked at me and gave a little smile:

'Don't educate them, Ken, don't educate them.'

"I knew what he meant. They were the best team in Europe and doing it their way. If the other clubs wanted to go down the road of coaching as the be all and end all, Bob didn't see it as his job to put the football world to rights. I wish he had bloody educated them though.

"I remember once, I was up in Glasgow to watch a player at Celtic. After the game, Jock Stein came over for a natter. It was the only time I ever got to speak to him, but within five minutes I knew his thoughts were similar to my own. He talked about open, attacking football and footballers who could change things on the pitch. He didn't mention formations or diets once. I would have liked to have the chance to talk more with him, but I heard enough.

"It was the same with Brian Clough. Funnily enough, I'd captained an FA XI in a game at Old Trafford and Brian had played for us that night. I didn't know him other than that, but years later, he brought a team to Maine Road when I was trainer for Malcolm. As I was walking out, he came out of their dressing room. I wasn't sure if he'd remember me and you find yourself in that embarrassing position, where you're not sure if you should let on or not, so I kept on walking. He shouted after me; 'Not letting on then, Ken?' We had a brief word and we met up after the game for a drink and a talk. He was a real one-off, Cloughie, but look what he did at Derby and Nottingham Forest. Amazing really isn't it? But make no bones about it, he was a manager not a coach.

"What did all those great managers have in common? They were all good at man-management and getting the right blend of bloody good players. There's an awful lot of skill and knowledge involved in that, of course, but not one of them had a bloody magic wand with the word 'coach' on it. I'd like to know how many coaching badges that lot had between. Not too many would be my guess. I know that, nowadays, people have to get the badges to get work. I understand that. That's the way things are. I say good luck to 'em. Get your badges and then forget all the bollocks they've been filling your head with. Then try to learn every lesson you can, from people who've actually been there and done it.

"I remember that idiot, Charles Hughes, at the FA. All the bollocks he came up with about fuckin' POMOs (Positions of Maximum Opportunity). I couldn't believe they let him loose with all that shite, I really couldn't. That clown also came up with the observation that most goals are scored from moves with three passes or less. So what? Are you really asking me to believe you would learn more in a week talking to that fool, than you would in half an hour with Shanks, Joe or Cloughie? No way.

"I really can't believe that people fall for all that rubbish. If you watch a good bricklayer or a good plasterer at work, it's great to watch. They make it look so easy. That's what craftsmen do; they make their craft look easy. But are you telling me that some clown, who's never laid a brick in his life, can watch a brickie, work out what he's doing and then teach someone else, who's also never laid a brick, how to do it? Can he balls. Why should football be any different? Good players make the game look easy, because it is to them. That doesn't mean that Charles Hughes, or any other bugger who's never played, can watch a game, break it down and then tell others how to play. It's an insult to your intelligence.

"We were talking before about Brian Clough. A total one-off, as I said. Was he concerned with POMOs? Was he bollocks. His skill, his genius even, was getting the best out of players, especially ones that other people were ready to write off. Look at the service he got out of players like Kenny Burns and John Robertson. Nobody else would have given them a second look. Cloughie had them up there with the best. Tell me this - how much of that was coaching and how much was good management?

"Another thing, when you think of all those great managers, remember how many good wingers they had playing for them. Matt had George Best, Joe had Mike Summerbee, Jock had little Jimmy Johnstone at Celtic. Peter Thompson at Liverpool and, later, Steve Heighway. John Robertson at Forest. Giggs and Kanchelskis for Alex. Wingless Wonders my arse.

"I know I go on about it, but over the years, coaching and all the shite that surrounds it, has been the bane of my life. Sometimes, it has made my blood boil, it really has. Other times, it's made me laugh. I'll never forget being at Maine Road once and Malcolm Allison was out on the pitch with Frank Carrodus and another young laddie. Fuck me, they were out there for ages. When they came off, I asked Malcolm what he'd been doing:

'I've been teaching them how to time a run, Ken.'

'Time a fuckin' run? If they can't time a run, what are they doing as professional footballers?' For fuck's sake, Malcolm, the only chance you've got is if you tie a piece of string to their bollocks. Then, when you're sat on the bench and you think they should make a run, give it a tug. Even then you wouldn't be quick enough, because the decision to go is a split second thing. By the time you pulled the string it would be too late anyway! Teaching them to time a fuckin' run. You have to laugh or you'd cry, you really would.

"I can also remember watching Malcolm work with Michael Robinson, who he'd paid stupid money for to Preston North End. I'd had a look at Michael and, in a lot of ways, he was an old style, robust centre-forward. My recommendation was that he would be worth getting, if the price was around the £100,000 to £150,000 mark. Bloody hell, they ended up paying out closer to a million for him. I'll never forget, I was talking to my scouting partner, John Doherty, who had played for United in the 1950s, but who's a mad keen City fan. John's a great scout, but he says what's on his mind, a bit like myself I suppose. We watched Malcolm with the lad for ages and it was obvious they were both getting a bit hot under the collar. John asked Malcolm what he was trying to do. Malcolm said he was teaching him to trap the ball with the outside, rather than the inside, of his foot. John looked at me and back to Malcolm and just said, 'How the fuck are you going to teach him that, when you can't do it yourself?'

"He was dead right. Malcolm and John go back a long way, to when Malcolm first came to Manchester. John had a club in Bowdon back then and had helped Malcolm, when Malcolm didn't have a pot to piss in. So Malcolm knew that John didn't mince his words. Maybe Malcolm thought John was just being John, but what he said was spot on. I don't suppose Malcolm took much notice though. He'd turned into the coach with knobs on by then. You really didn't know whether to laugh or cry sometimes."

One of Manchester's best known football characters, Fred Eyre, thinks that Ken is right about coaching in relation to the top players:

"Coaching probably doesn't apply to the great players. You can't teach the things that make them great, but I do think coaching can help average players to make the best of what they have."

Last word to Ken:

"I have to laugh when I hear players going on about 'great coaches'. It just means they try to make training more interesting. In Germany, you have to have played pro football to get your qualifications. Over here, anyone, from schoolteachers to bus drivers, can get on a coaching course. I don't want to be unkind, but how can that make sense? How can you teach what you can't do yourself?

"I believe there are certain qualities that go to making a good player. Those qualities include natural ability, control, skill, improvisation, anticipation, imagination, vision, guile, craft and having eyes up your arse. You are born with these qualities and you learn and improve with practice and experience. You hone your gift from being a kid into adulthood. But make no mistake about it, all the qualities I've just listed, are at total odds with modern coaching. Over the years, coaching has been so pedantic. All the emphasis is on systems and work rate. Keep it simple. Play the way you're facing. Push up to the half way line. Regimentation. If you don't concede a goal, you don't lose the game. What about winning and entertaining people? Don't you think it's strange that coaching has nothing to do with the things that make a player watchable? A lot of great players have never got involved with coaching. Maybe it's because they were such good players, that they understand that you can only help or advise. You cannot pass on or teach quality. No-one will ever convince me that, just because he's got a few badges and certificates, a bus driver can turn a Sunday league player into a pro. That is just shite."

KIDS

Throughout his many years as chief scout at Manchester City, Ken Barnes was responsible for bringing an array of young talent to the club. Ken's own experience as a young player trying to make a career in the professional game had been stark. Sink or swim. A quarter of a century later, Ken had very strong beliefs about the atmosphere he wanted to create and about how youngsters should be treated:

"The world had changed. Good youngsters, certainly the very good ones, might have half a dozen clubs on their trail. When the young boys came to City, I wanted it to be special. Not just for them but for their parents as well. I encouraged the senior players to call up for a chat and a drink with the boys and their parents. Denis Law was working in the media and he used to call and see me most weeks. It caused a few dads' jaws to drop when they walked in and saw Denis sat there, I can tell you. Even though I knew some of the boys would be looking at other set-ups, I never criticised other clubs. I wanted to convince them that what we had was special. I believed that if all the clubs were promising the boys the earth, the feel of a place could be the deciding factor.

"I remember walking into the treatment room once and the physio was massaging a young lad's bruised calf muscle. The boy had his foot on the physio's chest. He told the lad to come back and see him when he was back in next week. When the lad said he couldn't come back, because he was going to Villa next week, the physio dropped his fuckin' leg!

"I collared him later. 'What the shit are you playing at? Make it right for them.'

"Generally speaking though, I was pleased with the way we had things. I had a good team of scouts. My job officially ended once a lad had signed, but I always took an interest in how they were getting on, always. I remembered what it had been like for me as a kid. Nobody told you anything. It was a harsh world and, in some ways, that was no bad thing because you grew up fast or you went under. But the world changes and kids have to be handled differently nowadays. Bloody hell, I'm no softie, but I can remember Tony Book tearing a strip of one of the Beckfords. The laddie was only 17. I said to Tony afterwards, 'Fuckin' hell Tony, you must have been one hell of a player at 17. Didn't you ever make a mistake then?'"

The ability to spot a lad with real potential is one of the enduring fascinations of football. Ken Barnes has a track record to be more than proud of, so, what did he look for when assessing young players?

"The first thing that catches my attention is good control. A little bit of vision in his passing, is always a good sign and I always like to see a bit of tenacity. You can usually spot a thing or two. I know that, nowadays, clubs have 6 or 7 year old kids playing, but to be honest, I never really looked at anyone younger than 11. I don't know how the hell you're supposed to judge kids any younger than that. Of course, there's more to it than talent, character is vital too. It comes as a real shock for some lads. They've always been the best kid on the street and then they come here and everyone is the best on the street. It's not easy. Some thrive on it, some fall by the wayside, even some with real talent. Most take a bit of time to find their feet. I can tell you though, when they came here for the first time, I always told them the same thing - just to get out there and play. Don't worry about making a mistake, because everyone makes them, so just get out there and enjoy it.

"Sometimes a kid would come with glowing reports and be totally overawed. Some people would be telling me to get shut after 5 minutes. I always fought their corner. If the scout thought he was a good 'un, I trusted his judgement. I'd always invite them back. The number of lads who improved, beyond measure, on a second or third visit was unbelievable. If a lad signed, I always told everyone to forget about him for 6 months till he settled. It is a tough game, but you've got to at least try to give people a fair crack - that's what I believed then and I still do now."

If you are involved in the recruitment of youngsters, you have to be prepared for the inevitable 'one that got away' question. In the case of Ken Barnes, much has been written about his failure to sign Ryan Giggs for Manchester City. He is pleased to have the opportunity to put his version of events into the public domain:

"Ryan started coming to City at 13 or so and I knew pretty much straight away that he had the talent to play at a high level, no bones about it. I always knew him as Ryan Wilson and his father came to a few games at Maine Road and he used to come up to my office for a drink and a bite to eat. His dad used to play rugby league, as I recall. At the time, there were a couple of kids I was watching, who made you think they had a real chance of going to the top, Ryan and Michael Hughes. There wasn't a lot to choose between then at that age. I ended up falling out with Peter Reid about Michael a couple of years later, but, at that time, I knew they were both kids with that certain quality. Ryan's dad used to bring him down, like I say, and after a while I'd seen enough. I told his dad that there was a job waiting for Ryan at City when he left school. We shook on it and I believed it was a done deal. I always worked in the belief that my word was my bond and a handshake meant it was definitely settled. Ryan was on his way to City.

"A while later, Eric Mullender, a schoolteacher who did some scouting for me and who'd put me onto Ryan in the first place, told me the laddie had signed for United. I heard that his father had gone back to Wales and Ryan had taken his mother's maiden name and was now called Ryan Giggs. You didn't have to be Einstein to work out what had happened between his parents, but all my dealings had been with his dad. I was disappointed, of course I was, because I knew he could play and because I thought the handshake with his father had been worth something.

"Obviously, Ryan has gone on to have a great, great career with United and good luck to the lad. For my money, he is their most gifted player, no question about it. The one thing that really riled me though, was not losing out on signing him, because that happens, but what was said in Ryan's book. According to that, Ryan said that, even though he was a United supporter, he was expecting to sign for City. Apparently, when United came in for him he was surprised, but delighted, and wanted to sign right then and there. However, his mother insisted on coming to see me first, out of courtesy, to tell me that United were in for Ryan and to give me the chance to respond. Again, according to the book, I told Ryan's mother that I wasn't interested in signing Ryan for City. As a consequence, with honour served, they accepted United's offer.

"It's a lovely story of people behaving honourably. It's also absolute bollocks. Ryan's mother never came near me. In fact, to the best of my knowledge, I have never met her. So, it's a nice tale, but not true."

AN UNCERTAIN FUTURE

One area of the game which concerns Ken Barnes as much as any, is the finding and developing of young talent. The ultra professional approach of the top clubs nowadays and the advent of football academies would seem to suggest that the future is rosey. Not so says Ken: "I'd put a bomb under the academies. I said the same about Lilleshall when they first started that going. The idea may be sound enough, but it masks the real problem. Hundreds of schools don't bother with football anymore. Sport, especially football, used to be part of the school curriculum. That seems to have gone by the board. The schools used to be the first stage of the football filter. Then the boys went through area games to eventually reach Manchester Boys. What has happened to the lads from all those schools that are no longer part of the system? Have those boys disappeared? It all looks deceptively efficient. The schools of excellence and the academies - fine in principle. I have no problem with the basic concept, but if the raw material isn't there, you still end up with nothing much.

"They have kids as young as 7 attached to clubs these days. It sounds great, but to my way of thinking, they should just be out there playing without a care in the world at that age. If they start that young, the coaches just have more time to turn them into robots and play safe clones. They should just toss 'em a ball and say enjoy yourselves lads.

"There are no easy answers, because the world's a different place from the one I grew up in. Kids don't play like we used to.

We used to be on the streets unsupervised, for hours and hours. Society has changed so much. Parents are so scared of what can happen to their kids these days, it's easier to buy them TVs and computers and let them sit up in the bedroom. At least they know where their kids are that way. We played every day for hours. We practised without really knowing it. The raw material isn't there any longer. Look at Scotland. All the players that came from such a small country over the years. Not just good players, but bloody marvellous players - think about Bobby Johnstone and Denis Law at City for example. When was the last time you saw a Scottish player of that quality? Academies won't solve the problem.

"Maybe it has to be tackled at government level, to get football back into the schools. Trouble is, if you mention competitive sport these days, it goes against the politically correct grain. But the higher you go in football, the more competitive it gets. Teaching kids that competition is bad is not the start you're looking for.

"I've spoken to a lot of people I respect within the game about the academies. A lot of them agree with me that they are a waste of money. In fact, I was talking to one of the very top managers in the Premiership, who asked me what I thought about the academy system and knowing how much his club had invested, I thought I'd better pick my words carefully. I needn't have bothered. He let me squirm for a minute, as I tried to be honest but diplomatic, and then he described the academy system as a waste of time and money. They won't say it publicly, because the clubs have invested so much money in them. But it will be interesting to see what return they get on that money. I'm sure that some lads will come through the ranks, and the clubs will shout it from the rooftops to justify what they've spent, but in all honesty, I really do feel the problems start before the academy system kicks in.

"I'd love to offer a guaranteed solution, but the world really has changed and the breeding grounds of the game have shrunk. When I was a youngster, football was my obsession, but I wasn't unusual in that. If you walked round the streets of any town or city you would see games of football being played everywhere. That won't ever come back, so you'll have more clubs chasing fewer good players. Of course the odd gem will appear, but the base of the pyramid is still a lot smaller. I'd love to know the answer, or even if there is an answer. I'm not holding my breath."

THE PERFECT FINISH

In February 2005, Ken Barnes was inducted into the Manchester City Hall of Fame. It was a fitting tribute to a man who has made a phenomenal contribution to the club over more than half a century. It was a hugely popular award and at the celebratory dinner, Ken rose to say a few words to an audience made up of players, ex-players, officials and fans, spanning his 55 year involvement with the Blues.

Ken's assessment of his work, in all its varied guises?:

"Jack of all trades, master of fuckin' none."

Everybody laughed. Nobody believed it for a second.

EPILOGUE

As we come to the end of the book, let me say again, that it has been a privilege to help Ken Barnes record his memories of his time in football. As a keen Manchester City supporter it has been an absolute pleasure to spend so much time in the company of a man, who is part of the very fabric of the club I support. Over the past couple of years, it has been a source of huge interest to spend some considerable time talking to someone, better placed than most to give an insight onto a football age of which I have no real personal recollection: the 1950s. That harsh but endlessly fascinating era of Matthews and Finney, of Busby and the Babes.

In addition, Ken was also able to offer an insider's view of the incredible football roller coaster that has been Manchester City over the last 30 years.

When Ken asked me to get involved with this project, I admit to being more than a little daunted. Since leaving university back in the 1970s, I have written nothing more challenging than the odd newspaper article. I make no claims as a writer, but I have enjoyed being the recorder of a 50 year career in professional football.

As Ken looks back over half a century in the professional game, he has his doubts and concerns over the future of the game he loves. He is worried about the pervasive influence of coaching. Not the passing on of accumulated knowledge, but the belief that a coach can take any collection of would be footballers and turn them into a quality team. The footballing equivalent of alchemy; turning base metal into soccer gold. As intensive coaching becomes a fundamental part of the game at all levels, Ken believes, with a passion, that its influence will have the very opposite of its intended effect; that it will kill, rather than cultivate, real talent. Speaking of talent, Ken also believes that the supply lines of young players are drying up. As fewer schools play football and the kids are no longer playing and practising all the hours that God sends, neither schools of excellence nor academies are going to make up the shortfall. After nearly 30 years of working as a professional scout, a man who has signed more quality youngsters than most, is totally convinced that the pool of talent is shrinking and no amount of television and newspaper hype will make him think otherwise. Inevitably, there will be those who dismiss his doubts and consign him to the dustbin of football history. Just another old man who believes he played in some imaginary golden age. Another bitter ex-pro, stuck in a time warp, who refuses to accept the fact that the game is better than it has ever been. I would call for the defence a truly remarkable and highly impressive track record and the testimony of those who have known and worked with Ken Barnes over five decades in the professional game.

From my personal perspective, this book has been more fun than work - as you come to the end, I hope you can say the same.

THE LAST WORD

I want to thank, most sincerely, everyone has helped with and contributed to this book. It has certainly been an interesting exercise to look back on my life and I'm still wondering how the years could pass so quickly.

To be associated with a great club like Manchester City, for over half a century, has been a true honour. I have had some wonderful times and made many true friends during my time in football. There have been some dark times as well, of course, for me personally and for the club, but I wouldn't have missed it for the world.

Without wishing to tempt fate, the future is looking bright for the Blues and I want to express my thanks and best wishes to John Wardle and the board as they endeavour to take this great club onwards and upwards. I particularly appreciate the fact that they recognise that any club is the sum of many parts, including its past. The other ex-players and I are always treated as valued members of the City family, to be respected for our past contributions to the cause. We appreciate that respect and take great pride in our continuing allegiance to a very special club.

KEN BARNES
OCTOBER 2005

INDEX

The insider's to Manchester United
Candid player profiles of every post-war United player
by John Doherty
with Ivan Ponting
£20 - 364PP - PAPERBACK

Containing candid assessments on every United player to have appeared in a red shirt since the war, this magnificently illustrated work is penned by one of the few people to have seen nearly every post-war United player in action. Former Busby Babe John Doherty gives his honest opinion of the players he has watched down the years

The Birth of the Babes
Manchester United's Youth Policy 1950-57
by Tony Whelan
Landscape A4 Paperback
121pp - includes over 80 photographs

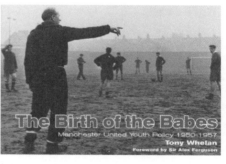

"I did not set out to build a team: the task ahead was much bigger than that. What I really embarked upon was the building of a system which would produce not one team but four or five, each occupying a rung of the ladder, the summit of which was the First XI."

MATT BUSBY

In The Birth of the Babes, current Manchester United Academy coach Tony Whelan examines not only the roots of Matt Busby's socialism, his approach to the care of his players, but illustrates the system of scouts, coaches and trainers that made Manchester United a prototype for the youth systems of today. Beautifully illustrated with photographs and memorabilia culled from the private collections of many of the youth players of the time, The Birth of the Babes is essential reading for anyone interested in the pre-Munich era when United took English football by storm.

CATCH A FALLING STAR
The Autobiography of Neil Young
£17.95 - Hardback - 224pp

A tall, leggy striker with a venomous left-foot shot, Neil Young scored in every significant game for City in the late 60s. For all the talk in the intervening years of the likes of Summerbee, Bell and Lee, it was the local lad made good who made the greatest impact when it mattered.

In Catch a Falling Star, Neil Young explains what he has been up to in the years since his sizzling shots stung the hands of the country's finest keepers. Here he frankly discusses the problem that faced footballers of the pre-Premiership era:

"When I left Rochdale for the last time one Friday afternoon I had a week's wages... about £60. I drove home and sat in my lounge for two hours, wondering what the hell I was going to do. I had a car on HP, a mortgage, a wife and three children to feed. I was the provider who could no longer provide. I had no savings whatsoever and my wife didn't work. I didn't see it coming. It was a calamity waiting to happen."

MY BLUE HEAVEN
by Dante Friend
18 GREAT GAMES, 18 GREAT NAMES

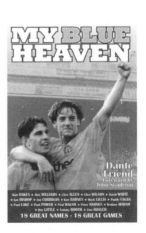

A collection of 18 interviews with star City men past and present including Rodney Marsh, Alan Oakes, Alex Williams, Mark Lillis, Uwe Rosler, Ian Bishop and Paul Lake.

RRP £10.99 - SPECIAL OFFER PRICE £8

This Simple Game

This Simple Game